From Commune to Capitalism

from COMMUNE *to* CAPITALISM

How China's Peasants Lost Collective Farming and Gained Urban Poverty

by ZHUN XU

MONTHLY REVIEW PRESS
New York

Copyright © 2018 by Zhun Xu
All Rights Reserved

Library of Congress Cataloging-in-Publication Data:
available from the publisher

ISBN: 978-158367-6981 paper
ISBN: 978-158367-6998 cloth

Typeset in Minion Pro

Monthly Review Press, New York
monthlyreview.org

5 4 3 2 1

Contents

Preface | 7

1—Socialism and Capitalism in the Chinese Countryside | 11

2— Chinese Agrarian Change in World-Historical Context | 19

3— Agricultural Productivity and Decollectivization | 39

4—The Political Economy of Decollectivization | 57

5— The Achievement, Contradictions, and Demise of Rural Collectives | 79

Epilogue | 109

Appendix 1 | 115

Appendix 2 | 119

Bibliography | 121

Notes | 133

Index | 149

Preface

I first came across the history of collectives and decollectivization in high school. My history textbook criticized the collectives and communes and praised decollectivization without any reservation. The illustrated post-collective peasants were dancing happily on the book. As I recall, I found the narrative and illustration in the textbook very persuasive. After all, thanks to decollectivization, we have all got enough rice to eat, right? My college major in economics later reinforced this view by providing a few jargon phrases. I believed that the Maoist period was an unfortunate disaster and, due to insufficient individual incentives under the collectives or other publicly owned enterprises, people at that time were lazy. So decollectivization and all the subsequent privatization reforms in China must have done great service to the working people.

It wasn't until later, when I had a chance to talk to relatives and friends who had spent their lives on a farm, that I began to doubt this view. None of them seemed enthusiastic about decollectivization. When I asked them, "Did you shirk under the collectives?" they would always say, "No, we worked day and night." I also noticed that in my very agricultural hometown, all the major infrastructure was built in the Maoist period, including a huge dam and big bridges. By contrast, no such projects were ever undertaken in the post-Mao era. It is clear to me that the gap between urban and rural and rich and poor is increasing. The villages are losing their vigor and the peasants are obviously not doing that well. My optimism about decollectivization and other neoliberal reforms has gradually shattered.

After college I came to the United States to pursue a PhD in economics at the University of Massachusetts Amherst. At the same time, I started reading many writings of Mao Zedong, as well as many other radical works on China. I was not alone. Quite a few graduate students at UMass Amherst were very interested in studying China's past and present from a revolutionary point of view. We had intense weekly discussions based on a wide range of Marxist writings. Zhaochang Peng, another graduate student, introduced me to several books by William Hinton, including *Fanshen*, *Shenfan*, and *The Great Reversal*. These books provided invaluable insights and inspired me to study the dramatic history of agrarian change in China.

During those discussions, I decided to write a dissertation on China's agrarian change, believing that it would be useful in the struggle for a better society. In China, the story of decollectivization is being employed as a strong ideological weapon to defend privatization and the free market. As soon as the issue of socialism and collective agriculture is raised, some people simply say, "We've done that and it failed. That is why we had decollectivization." For Marxists and socialists in China, it has become necessary to debunk the myth around collectives and decollectivization before they can convey their radical visions of a new society. I hope this book will contribute to those debates and struggles.

Many people provided immense help when I was working on this book, which is largely based on my PhD dissertation. David Kotz, Mwangi wa Githinji, Deepankar Basu, and Sigrid Schmalzer were on my dissertation committee and gave me numerous comments and suggestions. Over the past decade, I have also benefited from my many discussions with Ying Chen, Zhongjin Li, Shuang Wu, Kai Yu, Zixu Liu, Li Gu, Zhaochang Peng, Minqi Li, Hao Qi, An Li, Zoe Sherman, Chen Zhang, Rod Green, and my parents. I would also like to thank all my students and colleagues in China and the United States who have provided much feedback over the years. Many friends and relatives in my hometown have generously helped with my fieldwork. Last but not least, I would like to thank Michael Yates and Martha Cameron for their careful editing.

Much of this book has appeared in article form in several journals. Chapter 2 is based on "Chinese Agrarian Change in World-Historical Context," *Science & Society* 78, no. 2 (2014): 181. Chapter 3 is based on "The Chinese Agriculture Miracle Revisited," *Economic & Political Weekly* 47, no. 14 (2012): 51–58. Chapter 4 is based on "The Political Economy of Decollectivization in China," *Monthly Review* 65, no. 1 (2013): 17. Chapter 5 is based on "The Achievements, Contradictions and Demise of the Rural Collectives in Songzi County, China," *Development and Change* 46, no. 2 (2015): 339–365. I would like to thank the editors and publishers of these journals for their permission to publish slightly revised versions of the papers here.

1

Socialism and Capitalism in the Chinese Countryside

The nearly seventy-year history of the People's Republic of China can be roughly divided into two periods: during the first thirty years the PRC mainly followed the socialist path, but in the last four decades China has gradually become a champion of capitalism. As the Chinese maxim says, "Thirty years east and then thirty years west," meaning there is no eternity of ideas, powers, and social relations. The differences between the two eras are more than clear to the Chinese people. In 1949, Mao Zedong, the founder of the republic, proudly announced, "The Chinese people have stood up!" But nowadays, folk wisdom laments, "Work hard for decades, go back to the time before liberation in one night!" Every single aspect of social relations in China is marked by the retrogression from state socialism to capitalism. Everything has seen a great reversal. Red becomes black, noble becomes vulgar—and revolutionary becomes reactionary.

This book investigates some of these changes as they have affected land use and agriculture. In the 1950s, the PRC implemented a program of massive land reform and redistribution. The resulting collectives and people's communes worked for more than twenty years and made significant contributions to the country's economic development and to the education and health care of hundreds of millions of people. In the early 1980s, however, the Chinese Communist Party (CCP) undid much of the previous reform and dismantled the rural collectives, turning them into atomized peasant households while maintaining collective ownership of the land on paper. At the same time, academia and the mainstream media started condemning collective agriculture and praising the post-collective small-producer agriculture—formally called the house responsibility system, or HRS—as an alternative to collectives and capitalist farms. The actual performance of HRS, however, has been mediocre at best. Rural health care and education have clearly deteriorated as a consequence of decollectivization. Gains in agricultural production since the 1980s have been rather limited, and the gap between the urban and rural economies has become much larger than it was thirty years ago. Recent evidence also suggests that land consolidation and capitalist farms have developed rapidly in recent years, with the open endorsement of the CCP itself.[1]

Agrarian relations in China seem to have come full circle in just a few decades. The obvious question is, why? What historical forces led to a rapid decollectivization and a gradual path to capitalist agriculture after twenty years of collectives?

A simple but not uncommon explanationis the power struggles of the CCP leaders: the organization of agriculture in China is largely the result of the personal beliefs and triumphs of Mao Zedong and Deng Xiaoping and their respective allies.[2] These studies correctly point to the close link between CCP politics and agrarian change. However, they tend to focus entirely on individual political figures and their pursuit of power, which often leads to no more than detailed descriptions of palace intrigues.

Most existing studies look at the systemic changes in Chinese agriculture only through the lens of Chinese history, implicitly assuming a kind of Chinese exceptionalism. Such a narrow focus weakens our understanding of the significance of these changes. This book provides an alternative approach: placing the power struggles of the leadership and the consequent agrarian changes in China within the context of systemic changes that were happening concurrently throughout the globe. Analyzing the historical context does not necessarily imply a causal relationship; rather it shows that when countries face the same agrarian questions and constraints, they choose solutions that suggest certain general patterns.

As chapter 2 argues, recent trends in China have been more or less the same as in the rest of the world. The first three quarters of the twentieth century were marked by revolutionary changes in social relations. The driving forces were twofold: the worldwide socialist movement, beginning with the Mexican Revolution of 1910 and the Russian Revolution of 1917, and the national independence movement that followed the Second World War. The last quarter, however, was characterized by worldwide waves of privatization and deregulation, which are sometimes referred to as neoliberalism. Agrarian relations reflected these changes globally: in the first phase they tended to be more peasant-oriented, but in the second phase the peasant-capitalist compromise that existed in many nations came to an end. All the countries that had previously adopted progressive agrarian reforms stepped back and undid small or large portions of those reforms.

During the twentieth century, several different solutions to the organization of agrarian social relations existed. The capitalist and socialist paths are the obvious ones, but the populist small-producer path was also important.

Many developing countries started to address the agrarian question by choosing noncapitalist paths in the first phase. Most of them at least tried to guarantee peasants' access to the land, and many enacted redistributive land reforms or even encouraged collectivization to build socialism. However, these countries started to move to the capitalist path in the second phase.

How does this framework help us understand the Chinese situation? Actually, there were very different answers to the agrarian question within the CCP. Three major debates on the agrarian question took place during the 1950s and 1960s. The first debate was between the socialist solution and the capitalist one, while the second debate was between the socialist and the populist small-producer paths. In the end, and third, the factions in favor of the capitalist and populist paths joined forces against the socialist faction in the CCP. What we can observe is that the anti-socialist coalition always had significant political power, so Mao's intervention and his personal charisma and authority played a crucial role in the pursuit of the socialist path in China. But after Mao's death, the anti-socialist coalition faced no more political obstacles. They soon took power and abandoned the socialist agrarian policies. In recent decades, the political and academic mainstream in China and in many third-world countries has managed to take socialism off the agenda. Now the neoliberal capitalist program (the right) and an essentialist populist program (the left) occupy the political stage.

Gone is a class-based analysis. Instead, the mainstream has provided a sophisticated and highly influential theoretical framework for understanding the historical changes in the countryside, built around two key concepts: efficiency and spontaneity. First, the literature argues, the Chinese rural collectives suffered from inefficiency, and decollectivization greatly improved agricultural productivity.[3] The 1959–1961 famine is sometimes cited as an important factor to explain the need for decollectivization.[4] And second, because of their dissatisfaction with the rural regime, the peasants spontaneously organized and collectively dismantled the old system.[5] This narrative fits nicely in the hegemonic neoliberal ideology, which emphasizes the holy connection between individual "free choice" and spontaneous order and economic efficiency. And it has become part of the cornerstone of mainstream ideology in China.

My own research, however, shows that these stories are often unreliable and misleading. On the efficiency question, let us take grain production as an example. The grain yield grew at 2.79 percent annually between 1956 and 1980, which was the collective period; but it only grew 1.09 percent between 1984 and 2008, in the post-collective period.[6] There was indeed a famine in the late 1950s and early 1960s; however, this did not necessarily mean the collectives were inefficient. In fact, annual grain production grew at 3.44 percent per annum during the prefamine collectivization years of 1953 to 1958.[7] After the famine, grain production regained pre-famine levels by 1965. The annual grain production growth rate between 1965 and 1978 was 3.51 percent.[8] The famine, occurring twenty years before the period of decollectivization, hardly served as a cause for the end of a well-functioning system.

A more nuanced and often technical version of the efficiency story emphasizes that the transition from collective to household itself produced great efficiency gains. That is, there is a cause and effect relationship at work. One of the most widely cited sources for this version comes from Justin Lin, a leading proponent of market-oriented reform who later became chief economist at the World Bank. Lin's research, employing long-term panel data at the province level, argued that almost half of the increase in output during the transition period was due to decollectivization. In chapter 3, I critically review the literature and in particular replicate Lin's research model. After adjusting for some simple data errors, Lin's main results totally disappear; the new results suggest that the impacts from decollectivization are negligible. I then argue that the legacy from socialist agriculture accounts for the most important part of the success of the transition period and has had a long-term positive impact on agricultural development even after decollectivization.[9]

On the spontaneity question, a widespread belief is that the collectives were inefficient, so the peasants themselves dissolved their own collectives. Even leaving the question of efficiency aside, this view is in immediate conflict with the very logic of decollectivization. As Bramall argued, if the peasants could organize their decollectivization in the way they are said to have done, then collective agriculture would have been a huge success and there would be no need for decollectivization.[10] To be fair, this is not to deny that there were singular cases of decollectivization in small groups; nevertheless, it is simply ahistorical to explain the majority of cases in this way.

My research in chapter 4 shows that the CCP was enthusiastic rather than passive in promoting the household model. The cadres faced immense political pressure to follow the guidelines of the central leadership. The mainstream view holds that those people who opposed decollectivization were local cadres who were afraid of losing control. But my research suggests that the cadres and a small section of the peasantry implemented and benefited from decollectivization, while most of the peasants were not enthusiastic, and even opposed decollectivization in some cases.

Based on the evidence, I argue that decollectivization served as the political basis for the capitalist transition in China, in that it not only disempowered the peasantry but also broke the peasant-worker alliance and greatly reduced the potential resistance to the reform. The political significance of rural reform for the CCP cannot be overstated, and this was exactly why the mainstream interpreted decollectivization as spontaneous.

But if decollectivization was not driven by efficiency and spontaneity, why did it eventually succeed without major resistance? What were the internal contradictions of the rural collective regime that facilitated (if not "led to") its demise?

My fieldwork in Songzi County, documented in chapter 5, offers insights on this question. I find that rural collectives had remarkable achievements. Many of them did experience shirking (work avoidance) and inefficiency, not because of egalitarianism but because of stratification—because of a cadre-peasant, manager-worker divide. The actual demise of rural collectives was mostly due to political pressure from the Communist Party. But the stratification contributed to peasants' passiveness in resisting the institutional change.

Stratification was at the root of unsatisfactory performance and was the focus of peasants' complaints during the collective era. Decollectivization, on the contrary, seemed to be able to destroy stratification by destroying the whole collective, which, in turn, sometimes generated better performance in what had been dysfunctional collectives. That was probably one of the most important reasons why most peasants accepted the new policy without serious opposition. The rising income due to the procurement price adjustment probably also contributed to peasants' faith in the new policies. Certainly, other factors, like propaganda efforts from the cadres,should not be overlooked.

But was decollectivization a genuine solution to the stratification? Logically, stratification is not an integral aspect of collectives per se. In fact, the socialist element of the collectives put some constraint on stratification, at least on income distribution, but there were no such restrictions once it was dismantled: decollectivization disempowered the peasantry and allowed even greater and more explicit stratification and eventually class division.

Taking all these factors together, this book provides an alternative framework for analyzing the dramatic transition from communes to capitalism in the Chinese countryside. I hope this discussion will be useful to anyone who is willing to learn from the great history of socialism, humanity's efforts to end what we might call our prehistory.

2

Chinese Agrarian Change in World-Historical Context

INTRODUCTION

The twentieth century was an age of both revolution and counterrevolution. The first three quarters of the century saw revolutionary changes in social relations, mainly driven by the worldwide socialist movement that spread after the founding of the Soviet Union in 1917 and by the national independence movement that erupted after the Second World War. The last quarter was characterized by worldwide waves of privatization and deregulation, sometimes referred to as neoliberalism. This dramatic cycle shaped many crucial aspects of social relations in the contemporary world, in particular the trajectories of agrarian change.

After the Second World War, many countries implemented agrarian reforms that sought to protect peasants to varying degrees from landlords and usurers. One key element of these policies was redistributive land reform. In some places—for example, South Korea and Taiwan—"land to the tiller" was implemented. Land redistribution was relatively well enforced, and most peasants became small commodity producers. In other countries, like Peru and Chile, agriculture was even partly collectivized. Countries like Egypt, with no significant land reform, at least tried to put a cap on land rent and place restrictions on the size of individual landholdings. In socialist states like China and Cuba, the agrarian reforms included collectivization—collective ownership of the land by the peasants—partly to prevent potential class differentiation in the new peasantry.

This period has been called "the Golden Age of land reform."[1] These agrarian reforms were unprecedented in human history, both in scale and in content. One of the crucial features of agrarian reforms of this period was the reformers' goal of attacking pre-capitalist, mostly feudal or colonial, relations; this was often called "modernization." In most countries, the peasants were seen as allies of reform in varying degrees, depending on each country's internal conditions, while feudal lords or other traditionally privileged groups were the targets. In other words, for the first time in history, factions of the capitalist class compromised with peasants on a world scale.

Keep in mind that the compromise was not static. On the contrary, it was as riddled with contradictions as any social formation and was constantly changing. For example, the capitalist class encouraged compromise with the peasants at the expense of landlords in East Asian countries, while at the same time it quickly crushed the progressive reforms enacted by Jacobo Arbenz in Guatemala. Internationally coordinated capitalists overthrew the Chilean government of Salvador Allende in the 1970s and quickly undid a large portion of the previous land reform. At the same time, they launched the Alliance for Progress, which encouraged Latin American states to institute land reforms. Capitalists retreated from the compromise only when they sensed that they needed to do so, but in general they kept it and peasants saw improvements in their lives, and peasants benefited from it.

At the same time, agrarian reform in many countries was often constrained, in part because of the bourgeois character of the reform, and peasant proprietors often turned against revolution. For example, in Peru during the early 1960s, rich tenants became reactionary after land reform; similar events happened in a number of other countries as well.² Specific factors, like the form of the state, also matter. In India, for example, although the state has tried to create conditions for capitalist development, the democratic form of the state and class alignment in the society limits the effectiveness of land reforms.³

Both political and economic factors created the capitalist-peasant compromise in the first place. The political forces came from both internal and external class dynamics. Internally, the peasantry usually served as an important force in the revolutions, and the demand for agrarian reforms was a major part of the mobilization campaign for independence or revolution. This was the case for the newly independent states and socialist countries. External pressure was also crucial, especially in capitalist countries where the agrarian reforms came mainly from above.

Given the strong global communist movement and the example of the Soviet Union, peasants became inspired or even mobilized by domestic communists. If the national bourgeoisie was not able to carry out reforms to appease peasants, then capitalists in the rich capitalist countries would intervene. This is what happened in the case of Taiwan, where, in the face of the appealing example of socialist China, land reform was carried out jointly by the U.S. and Taiwanese governments.

Economic factors also played a role in the peasant-capitalist compromise. First, prereform agriculture was inefficient, so changes in agrarian relations were likely to bring a higher growth rate and national self-sufficiency. Latin America's hacienda system was a typical example. However, in places like India, where some landlords had already adopted capitalist methods of production, the efficiency factor was not so important.⁴ Second, it was argued that a more egalitarian distribution of land would increase domestic demand; this obviously fit in with the industrialization objectives of most national governments. In socialist countries, the economic argument for collectivization followed a similar vein: collectivization would generate a higher growth rate, which would facilitate industrialization; and better industrial support would benefit agriculture in the long run.

The political and economic factors did not work in fixed ways across countries, but for the bourgeoisie and bureaucrats in developing countries, progressive agrarian reform was a matter of necessity, not choice. Ironically, TINA—there is no alternative, the slogan promoted later by former British prime minister Margaret Thatcher to justify neoliberalism—was included then as an organic part of the development packages that were accepted by most national governments. However, the capitalist-peasant compromise came to an end during the 1970s. As Table 2.1 shows, all the countries that adopted progressive agrarian reforms stepped back and undid small or large portions of the previous reforms. In 1992, Mexico, the pioneer in agrarian reform, changed its 1917 constitution to allow land sales.[5] In 1994, Cuba, as the residualsocialist state, introduced private agricultural markets and divided state farms into smaller cooperative units.[6] In 1983, Tanzania, which had instituted the radical collectivization known as Ujamaa in 1974, published a new National Agricultural Policy to encourage commercial farming and land consolidation.[7] The demise of the Soviet Union in the early 1990s and the rapid privatization that followed in Russia and eastern Europe needs no elaboration.

It is worthwhile to analyze the global political and economic forces at work during this period. Political factors can be divided into two groups, internal and external. Internally, as the independence revolution faded away and bourgeoisie dictatorship strengthened worldwide, the overall capitalist order survived and more or less stabilized. Such was the case in both Taiwan and South Korea, which both enjoyed rapid growth. In socialist countries the ruling elites gradually became more pro-capitalist.[8] Peasants as a revolutionary force were no longer needed. Instead, in both capitalist and socialist countries, the ruling class preferred a depoliticized peasantry. This set the ground for breaking down the previous compromise.

Externally, the once strong communist threat was not there anymore; the Sino-Soviet debate, the collaboration between China and the United States in the post-Mao era, and the eventual demise of the Soviet Union greatly undermined the socialist movement. The capitalist class was largely relieved of the necessity of keeping the previous compromise and soon began to fight back. This was manifested

TABLE 2.1: Agrarian Changes: Selected Countries

Country	Phase 1	Phase 2	Notes
Algeria	1962	1981	The state sold all its estates inherited from French colonizers; state farms were privatized in 1987.
Chile	1967	1973	Pinochet's military government returned 30% of expropriated land to former owners; 20% was sold.
Cuba	1959	1994	Introduced private agricultural markets; state farms were divided into smaller units.
E. Central Europe	1940s, 1950s	1989	Massive privatization.
Egypt	1952	1992	Secured tenure revoked.
El Salvador	1980	1992	Land titling and parcelization of cooperatives.
Ethiopia	1975	1991	Secured private investors' rights to the use of land.
Iraq	1958	1987	Privatization by leasing or selling state farms to the private sector.
Mexico	1915	1992	Individual titling and freedom to sell land.
Nicaragua	1979	1990	Land titling and privatization of state farms; restitution of lands that had been illegally expropriated.
Peru	1969	1980	Parcelization of cooperatives.
Soviet Union	1920s	1989	Massive privatization.
Syria	1958	1990s	De facto privatization by provisioning tracts of state-owned land to agricultural companies.
Tanzania	1975	1983	Encourage commercial farming and land consolidation.
Vietnam	1940s	1980s	Decollectivization and free market.

Sources: El-Ghonemy, 1999; Kay, 1998; Mathijs and Swinnen, 1998; Metz, 1988; Daley, 2005; Barraclough, 1991; de Janvry, Sadoulet, and Wolford, 1998; Bush, 2007; Akram-Lodhi and Haroon, 2007; wa Githinji and Mersha, 2007; Hinnebusch, 1995.

ideologically both in academia—the decline of the Keynesians and the rise of the Milton Friedmanites, for example—and in the policies of such entities as the World Bank and the IMF. It was also enforced militarily if need be, as, for example, in the coup in Chile.

The economic forces were also significant. First and foremost, for a variety of reasons many agrarian reforms failed to deliver the high growth rate the reformers once expected. Governments in Latin America failed to provide financial, technical, and other support to agriculture.[9] Instead industrial accumulation often had a negative impact on internal terms of trade (price of agricultural goods relative to industrial output). In collectivization, it was common to have inexperienced leadership and poorly developed plans. In extreme cases, like the Soviet Union, grain production did not reliably exceed pre-revolution level until the 1950s.[10] It did not take too long for the ruling classes to conclude that the reforms were not productive enough. Second, the debt crisis broke out in many developing countries after the American interest rate hike in the early 1980s, which left indebted national governments unable to finance agrarian reforms.[11] Third, with the so-called green revolution starting in the 1960s marked by usage of high-yield varieties and chemical fertilizers, there seemed to be a technological alternative to the institutional reforms. Finally, global agribusiness also played a significant role. In some cases agribusiness directly demanded the reversal of the agrarian policies (as in Guatemala). On the other hand, after the 1970s, the unprecedented development of agribusiness and globalized food markets meant national capitalists could circumvent through trade and foreign investment the problem of food sufficiency and national industrialization, which marginalized peasants even further, both politically and economically.[12]

The gradual change in conditions led to a heightening of the inherent contradictions between the capitalist class and the peasantry. The peasantry remained silent and depoliticized, while the capitalist class became aggressive. The capitalist-peasant compromise became unsustainable, and this led to counterrevolution in the latter part of the twentieth century.

The Agrarian Question and China

The agrarian question refers to the transformation of the pre-capitalist countryside into a productive "modern" one: the development of capitalist or socialist relations of production in the countryside; the creation of surplus for national industrialization; and the role of the peasantry in political movements. Historically, this transformation has been accomplished in different ways. For the countries where small producers are prevalent in the countryside, there are three possible directions. The capitalist-oriented model tries to develop capitalism through differentiated peasant households. The socialist-oriented model develops collective production through organizing small peasants. The populist model tries to protect the small subsistence peasant households against commodity relations and capitalism, but without developing collectives. All these solutions agree on the need to abolish pre-capitalist agrarian relations, but they diverge after this very historical conjunction. While the capitalist path implies the development of the capitalist farmer and wage labor in the countryside, the socialist path means a significant degree of public ownership of land and other means of production; the populists in the classical sense reject both capitalist and socialist visions.

Many developing countries started to tackle the agrarian question by choosing noncapitalist paths in the revolutionary phase. Most of them at least tried to guarantee peasants' access to land, and many had redistributive land reforms or even encouraged collectivization to build socialism. However, these countries started to move to the capitalist path in the second phase. Former small-producer states like Egypt removed their protection of peasants; former socialist states like Soviet Union saw massive privatization and the emergence of capitalist agriculture.

How does this shed light on the agrarian changes in China? It is clear that the change in agrarian relations that we observed in China mirrored the general history of other developing countries. China had land reform and collectivization in the first phase and dismantled the collectives in the second phase. Although collective ownership of land is still preserved in legal terms, China has recreated small-producer agriculture through decollectivization. The rural economy is gradually becoming more oriented toward the market, and there is a clear tendency of further movement along the capitalist path.[13] Let us now look at how this change took place.

When the CCP first started the revolution in the 1920s, China was an extremely backward country marked by low productivity and a highly unequal distribution of land. It was widely accepted that 20 percent of the population owned more than 60 percent of the land. Between 50 percent and 70 percent of peasants' annual output went to the landlord as rent.[14] Unlike his peers, Mao did not see the peasants as passive—he saw in them the possibility of a dramatic revolutionary tide. He convinced his comrades of the importance of the peasant question, and the CCP finally took power because of the peasants' support. After the revolution, the CCP carried out extensive land reform nationwide and peasants became small landowners. However, the small plots and still existing pre-capitalist social relationships, not only just barely provided for peasants and their families but resulted in many farmers losing their land or ending up deep in debt because of illness, natural disaster, and other shocks inherent in the general backwardness of Chinese agriculture.

The CCP leaders agreed on the need to eliminate pre-capitalist relations, but they disagreed on the best solution going forward. Liu Shaoqi, then the second most powerful figure in the CCP, advocated for a capitalist-oriented solution. Liu once made the comment that small cooperatives cannot develop into socialist collectives and that the decline of cooperatives was good because it implied peasants were now better-off and could rely on themselves. Liu even quoted the example of Saint-Simon to argue that one can still be a socialist while being a capitalist.[15]

In the early 1950s, collectivization was not yet on the agenda, but in some places peasants spontaneously organized themselves into small cooperatives. Provincial leaders in Shanxi Province reported to Liu, suggesting that peasants should be further mobilized to build collectives; otherwise the rich peasants and exploitation would revive.

However, Liu was very much opposed to the idea of collectivization without a strong national industrial base and mechanization, calling such an idea "dangerous and utopian."[16] He even explained his vision of rural development: "now the countryside has class division, that is the basis of future revolution; in the future we can directly appropriate it [the new rich part of the peasantry]."[17]

At the same time, some other leaders preferred a more populist solution.[18] Deng Zihui, then the head of the rural work department of the CCP, was one of the outspoken members of this faction. Deng had a pessimistic view of peasants' "socialist consciousness" and argued that peasants preferred family farming to collective labor. He clearly disagreed with the capitalist solution, but he was skeptical about the socialist solution because of the lack of an industrial base and experience.[19]

In spring 1955, the relationship between the CCP and the peasants grew intense. Some peasants even commented that "the communists were worse than the nationalists."[20] At least two reasons were behind this attitude. First, new collectives were rapidly organized without sufficient mobilization and the middle peasants were afraid that their precious means of production would become publicly owned. Second, the state's grain procurement quota was so high that peasants did not have much left for their own consumption.

Deng Zihui believed that although the problem with grain procurement was significant, the fundamental problem was collectivization. He then pushed forward a policy of "contraction" in Zhejiang Province that aimed to dramatically reduce the number of collectives and the level of grain procurement. Within less than two months, the number of collectives had dropped sharply, by 30 percent.[21]

Unlike the previous two factions, Mao and his allies aimed to transform the agrarian relations by developing rural collectives. In an influential report, Mao laid out his arguments for collectivization.[22] First, as a response to Liu Shaoqi, he argued that agricultural collectivization served as the basis of mechanization, not the other way around. His rationale was that the mobilized and collectivized peasants could better resist natural disasters and manage their labor power and establish better conditions for the adoption of new technology and crop varieties. Collectivization would also increase peasants' purchasing power and thus increase demand for national industrial products. Mao also pointed out that the CCP would lose its political base among the poor peasants if they again suffered from the development of capitalism. He criticized Deng Zihui for overlooking the strong incentives of the poor peasants to work collectively owing to their lack of means of production. No single peasant family could afford or economically use a tractor, but a collective might be able to do both. Moreover, Mao critically examined the issue of "lack of experience," arguing that the peasants could only gain experience in building collectives by doing it themselves. Finally, the Soviet Union, the socialist state role model at that time, also gave important support to Mao's claim. Drawing on the Soviet Union's achievements after collectivization, Mao argued that collectivization was crucial for socialist industrialization and the development of agriculture itself. Mao further argued that the CCP could do a better job than the Soviet leadership by learning the lessons of its mistakes.

On the surface, these were merely different views on the sequence and pace of rural development, but they had profound political economy implications. Like Liu, many CCP leaders thought socialism and collectivization would come in the distant future, and they did not want to develop it until they felt its historical necessity. Implicitly, they were assuming the countryside had to go through a capitalist transformation before it became socialist.[23] Other people, like Deng Zihui, wanted neither capitalism nor socialism and preferred to stabilize the petty-producer economy.

These pro-capitalist and populist views actually gained significant support from the new Chinese elites. In the early 1960s, after the failure of the Great Leap Forward, most of the central leaders supported decollectivization.[24] It was estimated that 20 percent of the rural population adopted varieties of private household farming.[25]

This time, the pro-capitalist and pro-populist factions seemed to march hand-in-hand. Liu Shaoqi was very pessimistic and predicted that grain output under collectives would decrease for a long time.²⁶ Deng Xiaoping, who became national leader after Mao's death, was also in favor of decollectivization; he claimed that it should be officially encouraged nationwide, while collective agriculture must be "pushed back enough."²⁷ Deng also made the famous claim that "It doesn't matter whether a cat is black or yellow [usually "white" in English quotations of Deng], as long as it catches mice." In other words, it did not matter what method is used as long as it works.²⁸ The whole reform package implemented by these leaders was later called *sanziyibao*, which promoted private household farming.²⁹

Mao defended the rural collectives. First, he argued, grain production under the collectives began to recover in 1962, which was much sooner than the pessimistic expectations. Second, Mao pointed out the growing polarization in several poor provinces that had adopted decollectivization, with some peasants becoming landless and others becoming usurers. It was in this context that Mao later commented: "Why do I regard *baochandaohu* [decollectivization] as a serious threat? China is an agricultural state. Once agrarian relations change, our socialist industrial base will shake. Urban production relations will change inevitably and polarization will grow rapidly. How could we communists defend workers and peasants?"³⁰

In the end, China pursued the socialist path like many other countries, despite the strong support of the nonsocialist path among the leadership. This was due to socialist politics and ideology (plus direct influence from the socialist bloc), the need for industrialization, and, finally, Mao's unquestionable authority. At one point, it seemed that "only socialism could save China." However, as in other countries, the nonsocialist path eventually ruled, and the Chinese proverb was ironically twisted to read "only China could save socialism."

FURTHER CONSIDERATIONS

As China pursued the socialist path, the three alternative solutions to the agrarian question were translated into two major factions in the CCP: those who wanted to continue developing the collectives (socialist path) and those who wanted to go back to the pre-collectivization stage (the historical intersection of capitalist and populist paths).

These solutions did not "fall from the sky": they appealed to different classes in Chinese rural society. In general, poor peasants and ordinary workers (the majority) were likely to benefit more from the socialist path, while the middle and rich peasants (potential capitalist farmers) and bureaucrats (potential capitalists) might gain more from the other models, as the later reforms partly illustrated.

As a matter of fact, the socialist model had remarkable achievements. Due to the introduction of technologies such as new crop varieties and better fertilizer as well as their rapid diffusion via collective-based networks in the countryside, agricultural production improved significantly.[31] Massive social welfare programs were set up in the collectives that greatly improved overall public health and literacy in the Chinese countryside.[32] Many peasants still had faith in collective production despite various problems with the existing models. In a widely read book on the history of Chen Village in China, the authors interviewed the people in the 1970s who fled to Hong Kong from the mainland illegally. Many of these people, despite their flight, remained convinced that socialist agriculture was better than the private model and few of them felt hostile to the CCP.[33]

However, neither the achievements nor the potential support of the majority meant the state would necessarily pursue the socialist path. In Lenin's vision, under socialism, "there remains for a time not only bourgeois right, but even the bourgeois state, without the bourgeoisie!"[34] Mao's analysis confirmed Lenin's vision: "China now still has an unequal eight-grade wage schedule, equal exchange, allocation to one's labor, etc. It would be easy to launch capitalism."[35] Mao was correct. In Lenin's mind, the bourgeois state machine will be small and democratically controlled by armed proletarians; however, this was not the case in China (and most other socialist countries). Partly due to the influence of the Soviet model, China developed a large state machine with a strong, powerful, and conservative bureaucracy, which meant that there would be no democratic control of the state by workers and peasants.

Thus, the bourgeois state machine in China was able to develop its own interests and political power and reproduce itself by decreasing the power of workers and peasants. But within the state socialist regime, the party-state elites still faced various constraints on their personal wealth and power. Their income was much lower compared to their counterparts in the Western world, and they could lose their privilege anytime in consequence of the mass movements and intense political struggles that occurred.[36] Although there was no real bourgeoisie, the group that controlled the state machine had more than enough incentive to become one. The separation of the workers and peasants from the state also implied that the decision of development paths would largely be determined within the state machine, which tended to be pro-capitalist. That was why Mao used "capitalist roaders" to describe a significant portion of the upper-level cadres.

In the first seventeen years of the PRC, 1949 to 1966, these cadre, along with a portion of the elite workers and intellectuals, gradually established their control of the state. Although Mao and his allies resisted this tendency, which was parallel to that observed in the Soviet Union, they were not very successful. This constituted the major reason why Mao initiated the Cultural Revolution. It was only during the radical era (1966–1976) that the old state machine was partly smashed and Lenin's vision of democratic control of the state machine was partly realized. However, the Cultural Revolution did not successfully establish peasant and worker control of the state, and the old state apparatus was restored gradually in the 1970s.[37]

Since the anti-socialist coalition had significant political muscle during most of the time Mao was in power, his intervention and personal charisma and authority played a crucial role in the pursuit of a socialist path in China. Sometimes it even seemed that Mao just by himself overturned the bureaucratic state machine.

Partly as a prophecy, the famous 1975 movie *Breaking with Old Ideas* (*Juelie*) told a story about collective versus private farming. The socialists had the popular support of the rank-and- file CCP members and most of the peasants, but they lacked political power. The capitalist roaders had the support of rich peasants, but most importantly, they were supported by the majority of the local CCP cadres, who received underground instruction from top central leaders. The socialists lost the political battle. They were forced to leave their positions and were even jailed. It looked as though decollectivization was going to happen when Chairman Mao directly intervened, writing a letter to show his full support for the socialists. In the end, the capitalist roaders were defeated and sunshine came back to the countryside. However, if we follow the movie's logic, without Mao's intervention, decollectivization would have been inevitable, given the political structure.

And this was exactly what happened after Chairman Mao died in 1976. There were no major obstacles for the anti-socialist coalition, and the palace coup just added some novel flavor, although it still took some years for them to figure out how to destroy Mao's legacy.[38] Interestingly, *Breaking with Old Ideas* was banned three years after Mao's death and was condemned as "poisonous weeds."[39] Starting from the early 1980s, the CCP implemented nationwide decollectivization despite considerable resistance from the peasants and local cadres (for more details see chapter 4). The Chinese peasants, now forced away from the socialist tradition, returned to the status of small producers.

Most working people did not immediately see the implications of all these change for themselves. But artists often did. Only seven years later, in another highly influential film, *The Herdsman* (*Mu Ma Ren*), a poor herder is talking with an intellectual who had been a herder in Mao's era and became a teacher in the post-Mao era: "You were once among us; now we folks are all done."[40]

THE STORY CONTINUES IN THE NEOLIBERAL AGE

The triumph of the anti-socialist camp has marked the start of a new era, with socialism semiofficially taken off the political agenda. Nowadays the post-Mao leaders repeatedly claim that China will "never go back to the old road."[41] Yet what will the "new" road be?

With the socialist solution now considered politically incorrect, all that remains is populism and capitalism. An abrupt transformation from socialist collectives to capitalist farms would have been risky in the 1980s, since it might have stirred serious doubts from the masses, created landless peasants, and nurtured political unrest. Therefore, at that moment, a populist solution, with stable small landownership and family farms, seemed more feasible. The decollectivization campaign began in the late 1970s, although it was camouflaged under the guise of "socialist development." But it actually took the Chinese countryside back to the pre-collectivization historical compromise between populist and capitalist factions that existed in the early 1950s.

If the populist camp in the Mao era was only arguing for a relatively gradual transition to socialist collectives, their contemporary counterparts were looking to something different. Given the changes in the overall political economy, the populist solution was now more aligned with capitalism. In essence, this type of neo-populism or pro-market populism portrays a homogenous peasantry with a strong preference for family business and the market.

The ambiguous dividing line between the two factions found its best example in Du Runsheng, the architect of the new agrarian relations and then-head of the National Agricultural Committee.[42] Du argued that given the uniqueness of Chinese agriculture—which was "sensitive," "vulnerable," and "undermechanized," in his words—small producers would take better care of the crops than collectives could. In a report published in the *People's Daily*, Du claimed that "the contemporary world" has proved that family farming is perfectly compatible with modernization.[43] Clearly, this "world" only referred to the United States and Western European countries. In his later years, Du admitted that his ideas came partly from his positive impression of the United States, Japan, France, and other developed countries that he visited after 1979, in particular the widespread presence of family farming and modern technology.[44]

Despite the seeming superiority of small family farms over all other forms of agricultural production, in Du's argument, the populist solution did not preclude a gradual transition to large-scale capitalist agriculture. As Du himself emphasized in the same report, "we do not want to maintain petty production forever; we will move on to big modern production."

Only a few years later, Du revisited the question of agrarian change, adopting an even more pro-capitalist stance. In his speech at the CCP's Central Party School, Du openly criticized family farms for their inefficiency and claimed that Chinese agriculture should develop economies of scale.[45] However, Du denied the advantage of developing collectives, claiming that "the peasants would not support collectives." Du's argument implies only one choice: capitalist farms. In line with his idea, Du later made several policy suggestions, including transferring rural labor to urban industries and encouraging gradual land concentration to the advantage of fledgling capitalist farmers.

Soon after the decollectivization campaign, the honeymoon between the populist and capitalist factions came to an end. The scholars and policy makers in the capitalist faction mainly focused on the development of capitalist relations of production in the rural areas (that is, "efficient scale farming"), and they often tended to overlook the suffering and dispossession of the small peasant families during the process. The national policy became more urban and industry-oriented after the mid-1980s; the rural-urban income gap increased dramatically; and public investment in rural areas dropped significantly from the level of the Maoist period.[46] In 1999, a local cadre, Li Changping, wrote a famous letter to Premier Zhu Rongji, stating that "the life of the peasants is extremely hard, the rural areas extremely poverty-stricken, and the prospect of agriculture extremely precarious."

Those on the populist side do not oppose capitalism in principle, but they are more cautious about its disastrous impacts and, to some extent, represent its humane side: equal rights for urban and rural residents, tax cuts for peasants, price protection for agricultural products, and other welfare policies for the countryside. In the view of Wen Tiejun, a leading scholar in the populist camp, the Chinese intellectual should "deconstruct" the concept of modernization in order to protect the "unavoidable" petty peasant rural economy.[47]

The split redefined the mainstream political spectrum from the 1980s onward. On rural issues, the supporters of the capitalist solution became the right wing, while the populist opposition—however mild—formed the left wing. Sometimes, the populists and socialists have even found common ground in opposing policies of the capitalists. For example, on the issue of land privatization, those supporting socialism strongly defend the last remaining legacy of collectivization; the capitalist faction favors complete rural land privatization to facilitate land concentration; and the populist faction favors a more gradual approach and also supports maintaining a de jure collective ownership of land to protect the de facto small ownership.[48]

The contemporary historical process of agrarian change could be understood as a dynamic compromise between the populist and capitalist factions but with heavier weight on the latter. Since the beginning of this century, the populists, claiming that they represent the voices from below, have succeeded in persuading the central government to provide certain welfare supports and tax reductions for rural residents.[49] Yet the capitalist faction, representing "efficiency" and "advanced forces of production," has also won the upper hand on crucial issues. For example, the Third Plenary of the CCP's 17th Central Committee in 2008 passed a resolution on rural development that explicitly encouraged peasants to trade land use rights to concentrate land for more large-scale efficient agricultural production.

Despite any possible differences, the two factions share in common the denial of any socialist rural project. After all, the populist faction does not really oppose the market and capitalism, and the capitalist faction is not arguing for the immediate abolition of small producers.

Again, the political subtlety in China in the second phase has found its counterparts and connections in other countries, although often in a twisted way. According to Brass, the rhetoric of the latter half of the twentieth century held that the new rural movements in Latin America and other developing countries abandoned the means of mass mobilization and the goal of socialism.[50] As for the actual ongoing highly political and anti-neoliberal peasant movements in Mexico, Brazil, and other countries, Petras and Veltmeyer note that the mainstream either perceives the movements in recent decades as premodern, arguing that the homogenous peasantry was fighting a losing battle; or treat the struggles as postmodern, seeking cultural and ethnic identities.[51] In fact, Chinese intellectuals like Wen Tiejun also explicitly refer to these movements as evidence of support for the populist notion of a homogenous above-class peasantry. As in China, the political and academic mainstream in other third world countries has managed to take socialism off the agenda, leaving the neoliberal capitalist program (the right) and a populist program (the left) to occupy the political center stage. Keep in mind that the two visions are not mutually exclusive. To paraphrase Brass, neoliberalism accepts small peasants as long as agricultural goods are produced efficiently for the market.

If we consider the overall effect of agrarian change, we can find its entanglement within the larger global context of neoliberalism. Decollectivization and the changes that followed led to the largest migration in human history, creating a new working class for the urban industries (the number of migrant workers was more than 280 million in 2016).[52] This huge reserve army further disempowered the old urban working class and facilitated the massive privatization of the last two decades. Globally, the world labor force saw a significant expansion in the last few decades, owing to the radical reversal in agrarian relations: depeasantization in the peripheral countries by means of agribusiness as well as integration of the labor force in former socialist states into the world economy.[53] Obviously, the increase in the global reserve army greatly contributes to the power of the world capitalist class and plays a crucial role in the neoliberal order. And Chinese agrarian change has been an integral part of the entire process.

CONCLUDING REMARKS

China's changing agrarian relations have always been an important part of the world-historical process. In the Maoist era, the struggle was primarily between the pro-collective (socialist-oriented) faction and the anti-collective (both capitalist and populist-oriented) faction. In the post-Mao era, the tensions within the anti-collective camp have taken center stage, with their resolution largely in favor of capital. The pattern in China shares similarities with other countries, but it has its particularities, mainly owing to Maoist radical policies.

As we can see, since the end of the Maoist era, China has been gradually integrating itself into the contemporary capitalist world, not only in economic terms but also politically and in terms of scholarly work. In other words, contrary to mainstream claims of "Chinese exceptionalism," China has, in fact, become more and more "normal" compared to other developing countries in terms of agrarian relations (and overall social relations) as it has digressed from Maoist radicalism.

With decollectivization and further neoliberal reforms, the current Chinese state faces a dilemma in representing capitalist class interests and simultaneously maintaining legitimacy among peasants and workers. On the one hand, the dominant interests of the urban capitalist class and the multinational businesses require a consistent supply of workers and land, thus implying the further consolidation of rural land and development of capitalist relations. On the other hand, the government needs to appease the peasants and workers by protecting them from dispossession and sweatshops. Another aspect of the state's legitimacy concerns is the need to guarantee a high level of food sufficiency. China's increasing food demand is so large that it cannot be met by international food market, which contributes to the state's hesitancy in pursuing any dramatic changes in the countryside. The result of this dilemma remains to be seen, but the chance of a peaceful solution is slim. China could find itself in both political and economic crisis if the labor supply begins to decrease and labor's bargaining power begins to increase, or if the state cannot address the concerns of the working class.

Future socialist projects can draw at least two lessons from Chinese agrarian history. First, without democratic control of the state by the workers and peasants, the already challenged socialist project (or any progressive project) will be even more fragile. This has been the case with China and many other countries that have gone the full circle in their agrarian relations. Second, the struggle for socialism is a long-term project, with contradictions and opposition along the way. When the Chinese Revolution succeeded in 1949, Chairman Mao declared that we had only finished one step in the Long March. This is indeed so. To paraphrase an ancient Chinese saying, building socialism is like rowing against the current, and no advance means retreat.

3

Agricultural Productivity and Decollectivization

INTRODUCTION

The dismantling of the rural collectives in China began in 1979 and took five years to complete. By 1984, the transition to the household production system was firmly established, and it has remained stable since then. Although different studies have presented varying results, there is a general consensus that decollectivization is the most important reason for China's impressive agricultural performance in the early 1980s.

However, Chinese agricultural productivity slowed down significantly after the completion of decollectivization. Table 3.1 lists the growth rate of the yields of the three most important crops (grain, cotton, and oil crops), which constituted more than 80 percent of total sown area in both the transition period and the era of stable household production. For all three crops, the average yield growth rate decreased dramatically after 1984. It is thus fair to conclude that agricultural performance in the stabilized household production era was inferior compared to that of the transition period.

Since performance in the era of stabilized household production has not been impressive, what is the real source of the Chinese

TABLE 3.1: Household Agriculture before and after 1984

	% of total sown area			YIELD GROWTH RATE (%)		
	1970	1980	2008	Transition period	Stable household	First year 1984 level achieved
Grain	83.12	80.09	68.34	7.17	1.33	1987
Cotton	3.48	3.36	3.68	9.07	1.53	1997
Oil crops	3.15	5.42	8.21	13.20	2.18	1990
Total	89.75	88.87	80.23			

Source: Ministry of Agriculture, 2009, 17, 23, 25; State Statistical Bureau, 2005, section 39.

agriculture miracle during the transition period? To answer this question, it is necessary to reconsider the causes of the remarkable growth in the early 1980s. A critical review of the historical process and previous studies of this period indicates that decollectivization did not have a significant impact on output, while more intensive application of modern inputs and other exogenous factors, such as weather, accounted for most of the growth in output.

HISTORICAL OVERVIEW OF THE TRANSITION PERIOD

The transition period was complex, with very different forces in operation at the same time. While it is not possible to cover all the facets of change during this period, this overview offers an analysis of a variety of factors, from weather conditions to institutions.

Decollectivization: The Household Responsibility System

Before the reform, Chinese rural production and distribution were all managed by production teams, which were the basic units under the people's communes. During the early stage of reform, some management adjustments in the collectives were permitted, but the collective framework was maintained, and work management and income allocation were still determined by the collectives. One of the popular forms of this early transitional policy was that small jobs were contracted to workgroups or individuals with specific skills. But in fact, small-job contracting was not new at all: it had been practiced during the collective era. However, under the new regime, more economic incentives were used. That was why this policy was called the "responsibility system" (*zerenzhi*), or more accurately, the "performance-based compensation and responsibility system" (*lianchanzerenzhi*).

The early reforms of the collective system proved to be minor compared to the decollectivization reforms of 1980–1981, when collectively owned land was divided up among rural households, and production, distribution, and related business came under the full control of individual families.[1] This new policy basically dissolved the collectives and, from 1984 on, made the individual household the basis of the new system of production. This decollectivization reform was vividly named "divide-all-up" (*da baogan*), but it was later renamed the "household contract and performance-based compensation and responsibility system" (*jiating lianchan chengbao zerenzhi*), or simply, the household responsibility system (HRS) for short. As column 1 of Table 3.2 shows (see page 43), HRS expanded very rapidly: in 1980, only 14 percent of production teams had adopted HRS; two years later, 80 percent had adopted HRS.

Technology Diffusion and Conditions of Production

One of the remarkable features of the transition period was the intense use of chemical inputs. The application of chemical fertilizers had risen steadily from 1970 on, including during the last few years of the collective system as production capacity improved. This trend continued into the transition period, during which fertilizer application almost doubled in five years (Table 3.2, col. 2). Moreover, it has been noted that the Chinese agricultural system was severely nitrogen-constrained during the 1960s and 1970s. There was a significant improvement in the quality of the fertilizer during the transition period because the large synthetic ammonia-urea complexes imported by the central government in 1973–1974 (during the collective era) went into production in the late 1970s.[2]

The green revolution started in China during the collective era, and within a short time a nationwide agricultural research system was established that was "highly developed, broadly based, and sophisticated."[3] The spread of improved seeds (high-yield varieties) was particularly important for Chinese agricultural growth; as early as 1959, 80 percent of China's sown area was planted with improved varieties, but seeds were continuously improved throughout the collective era.[4] For example, hybrid rice was developed in the mid-1970s, but nationwide dissemination really coincided with decollectivization (Table 3.2, col. 3). Moreover, given the fact that the collectives had been building numerous water reservoirs and other rural infrastructure starting from the late 1950s, the dramatic increase in chemical fertilizer availability and quality in the transition period compounded the advantage of the hybrid varieties.[5]

Between 1970 and 1978 the use of agricultural machinery increased by more than 400 percent, thanks to a national goal of mechanization during the collective period (see Table 3.2, col. 4). This trend continued between 1978 and 1987, but at a more moderate growth rate of 8 percent per year. The relative decline during and after the transition period was not only due to the lack of state support for agriculture mechanization. It was also a natural outcome of HRS: individual households had little incentive to use big tractors and combines on their extremely small, scattered plots.

A significant determinant of agricultural output is weather. During the collective era, rural communities were able to construct numerous water reservoirs and dams to minimize the impacts of bad weather. Nevertheless, weather changes did matter for agriculture performance, particularly in the short run. An index measuring weather fluctuation from 1970 to 1987 is presented in column 5 of Table 3.2. The index was computed as a deviation from a long-term average; thus, higher numbers represent worse weather than average and lower numbers represent better weather. The calculations suggest that weather conditions were generally more favorable from 1970 to

Agricultural Productivity and Decollectivization

TABLE 3.2: Conditions of Production, 1970–1987

Year	HRS Adoption [1]	Use of Fertilizer [2]	Hybrid Rice Diffusion [3]	Machine Power [4]	Weather [5]	MCI [6]
1970	0	3,512		21,653	−73.72	141.9
1971	0	3,647		n.a.	−29.41	144.7
1972	0	4,207		n.a.	21.67	147
1973	0	5,111		47,829	−21.53	148.2
1974	0	4,858		59,303	−23.01	148.7
1975	0	5,369		74,786	−12.62	150
1976	0	5,828	0.4	86,296	1.55	150.6
1977	0	6,480	6.2	102,617	28.89	150.5
1978	0	8,840	12.6	117,499	53.61	151
1979	0.01	10,863	15.4	133,795	12.02	149.2
1980	0.14	12,694	14.2	147,457	47.4	147.4
1981	0.45	13,349	15.4	156,801	26.91	146.6
1982	0.80	15,134	16.8	166,142	7.74	146.7
1983	0.98	16,598	20.3	180,219	10.17	146.4
1984	0.99	17,398	26.7	194,972	2.69	146.9
1985	0.99	17,758	26.4	209,125	47.18	148.4
1986	0.99	19,306	28.3	229,500	54.346	150
1987	0.99	19,993	33.0	248,360	34.63	151.3

Notes: HRS adoption measures the year-end percentage of production teams that adopted the HRS. Chemical fertilizer is in thousand tonnes. Hybrid rice diffusion measures the percentage of total rice fields planted with hybrid seeds. Machine power is in thousand kilowatts. The weather index is a constant weighted sum of Shouzai and Chengzai areas. The weather variable presented here is the yearly percentage deviation of each year's index from 1952 to 1984 mean; more details can be found in Kueh's book.

Sources: Cols. 1 and 6: Lin, 1992. Cols. 2 and 4: State Statistical Bureau, 2005, section 38. Col. 3: Stone, 1988. Col. 5: Kueh, 1995; the 1985–1987 index is calculated based on Kueh's method.

1975; this period was followed by five years of bad weather. During 1980–1984, natural disasters became relatively smaller and less frequent; after1985 the weather again worsened on a national level.

Finally, Table 3.2, column 6, lists a commonly used measure of relative labor intensity known as the "multiple cropping index" (MCI). This index, whichis calculated as total sown area divided by total cultivated land, captures the change in relative labor spent on a unit of farmland. It kept increasing in the collective era because increased irrigation and mechanization allowed collectives to cultivate more intensively.[6] According to many defenders of HRS, peasants did not work as hard under the collective structure because it was difficult to monitor their effort. The multiple cropping index suggests just the opposite, however: the intensity of labor decreased in the transition period, although it seems to have been restored to previous levels after 1985.[7]

Procurement Adjustments

From the mid-1950s, China adopted a policy called "unified procurement and marketing" (*tong gou tong xiao*), which meant that the government had a certain monopoly power in terms of the purchase and pricing of agricultural output. All farm products were classified into three categories. The first category included strategic goods like grain, oil crops, and cotton. Goods in this category were subject to compulsory purchase by the government at a given procurement price. In 1972, a price premium of 20 to 30 percent was introduced for above-quota output; surplus product could be sold at a negotiated price, which was mostly higher than the above-quota price.[8]

Starting in 1979, there was a significant increase in procurement price for the first category, as well as for tobacco, live hogs, and sugar crops. For instance, the procurement price of grain was increased by 20 percent, and the price premium for above-quota output increased from 30 percent to 50 percent.[9] There were further price increases for certain crops. At the same time, the compulsory quota was gradually reduced; this continuously increased the average prices and profit margins (see Table 3.3, col. 1).

Two points need to be kept in mind regarding these procurement adjustments. First, if one does not consider the impact of the quota decrease on weighted price, it would appear that prices stagnated during the good harvest of 1983 and 1984; in fact, the profit margin *increased* until 1984. (Table 3.3, column 3, lists the average profit margins of the three main grain crops.) Second, the industrial input price also increased; hence, Table 3.3, column 3, the ratio of above-quota price to industrial input price, provides a more balanced view of the situation.

Some researchers also emphasized the function of reestablished rural markets during the transition period; however, the overall impact of marketization on agriculture during this period was arguably small, as can be seen from the percentage of grains sold on the market (Table 3.3, col. 4). Therefore, the impact of rural marketization is not considered in this research.

It is not hard to understand the impact of price increases on peasants' incentives; however, the exact degree of the price increase is hard

TABLE 3.3: Procurement Adjustment: 1978–1987

Year	Grain in Quota Sales (%) [1]	Main Grain Crops, Net Revenue [2]	Ratio of Above-Quota Price to Industrial Input Price Index [3]	Grain Sold on Market (%) [4]
1978	75	0.25	100.0	0
1979	58	2.81	140.4	7
1980	56	2.77	139.2	7
1981	44	3.05	142.3	7
1982	38	3.74	139.3	8
1983	29	4.35	138.6	5
1984	26	7.11	132.1	9
1985	73	7.19	116.2	16
1986	55	8.97	113.3	17
1987	44	7.92	108.1	21

Note: The main grain crops include cereal, wheat, and corn; this net revenue measures the after-tax profits from 50 kilograms of grain output on average.

Sources: Cols. 1 and 4: Aubert, 1990. Col. 2: State Development and Reform Committee, 2003. Col. 3: Lin, 1992

to measure because there were nationwide sales programs throughout this period to give extra grains or fertilizer for above-quota deliveries, not to mention various local programs of similar kinds.[10]

This is a brief illustration of the complicated conditions that pertained during the transition period. Some factors were counterproductive, while most seemed to be favorable for growth. Now we turn to an examination of the household responsibility system.

A CRITICAL ASSESSMENT OF THE IMPACT OF HRS

Most of the literature shares an unfailing faith in decollectivization and HRS (the two terms will be used interchangeably in this study). However, some more detailed and pragmatically objective studies have cast serious doubts on the acclaimed advantages of HRS. Among the pro-decollectivization studies, Justin Lin's work has been most widely cited, especially in government documents, although it is occasionally referred to anonymously as "some research." It is therefore necessary to provide a critical assessment of Lin's main findings.

Pro-HRS Studies

In this category, there are two main types of studies. The first focuses on total-factor productivity (TFP) in China's agricultural sector. Most of the studies suggest that TFP increased during the transition period, although some acknowledge that TFP decreased once HRS was fully established and stable, that is, after 1985.[11]

There are many ways to construct TFP (or its growth rate). For instance, a TFP growth rate may be calculated using a simple growth accounting exercise that extracts the weighted sum of the growth rate of certain key inputs from the output growth rate. A TFP index may also be generated simply by dividing the output by a weighted sum of input. In some studies, the TFP index has been calculated using more sophisticated methods, like the Divisia index and the Törnqvist-Theil index. In essence, TFP index construction tries to eliminate the contribution of inputs from output growth to get the portion that cannot be directly explained by all traditional inputs.

Leaving aside the problematic usage of TFP in the underemployed agriculture context (no precise labor input data), none of these studies provided convincing arguments regarding the role of HRS. First, their results show that TFP (or TFP growth rate) was generally higher in the transition period compared to the collective era. Without analyzing the existence of a causal relationship between HRS adoption and production, they explicitly or implicitly—and hastily—arrived at the conclusion that HRS was superior, not even asking whether HRS was an important factor at all. But as the last section showed, there were many different forces in operation during the transition; therefore, these studies failed to provide a convincing argument for the superiority of HRS. Second, in all of these studies, TFP figures tended to decrease in the post-1984 stable HRS period, yet the studies failed to develop a consistent framework to explain this decline. For example, some scholars tried to argue that the real procurement price decrease after 1984 partly explained the production decline, but they never mention the role of price increase in the transition period, which by their logic would account for the higher TFP then and not necessarily the HRS system.[12]

The second type of pro-decollectivization study directly tackles the issue of the role of HRS adoption in the transition period.[13] These studies try to differentiate the effects of HRS from other possible factors; nevertheless, they also suffer from a number of serious defects. The study by McMillan, Whalley, and Zhu is typical. These authors maintain that 22 percent of the increase in productivity in Chinese agriculture between 1978 and 1984 was due to higher prices and 78 percent to changes in the incentive scheme (HRS).[14] There are two major problems in this analysis. First, the authors assumed that HRS reform happened uniformly and instantly after 1978, when in reality it took a while for the political struggle to finish the reform (as Table 3.2 shows) and the adoption of HRS varied across localities (the authors do acknowledge this in the paper), so the increase in productivity after 1978 cannot be attributed simply to HRS. Second, the authors assume that no technical progress occurred during the reform period, which is not true.[15] As discussed above, there were several important technical changes (use of hybrids, better fertilizer) during this period as a result of efforts made during the collective era. Needless to say, the results also depended on their model setup, which adds another level of uncertainty to their results. Again, as a general comment, these studies fail to provide evidence for the superiority of HRS.

Pragmatic Studies

There have been pragmatic studies that tried to debunk the belief that HRS outperformed collective agriculture. Some researchers studied the general impact of HRS. Carolus concluded in her 1992 dissertation that the adoption of HRS was responsible for no more than 20 percent of the increase in total crop value if the most plausible set of input, crop mix, and year-specific factors is accepted. She also pointed out that the impacts of HRS varied with different preexisting conditions. But Carolus's work covered a very wide range of HRS impacts, so it was not able to give a clear overall assessment of HRS.[16] On the other hand, Riskin suggested that some of the increase in reported production represented production that had already existed but had been concealed before decollectivization.[17] Bramall doubted the fundamental validity of TFP calculation owing to lack of knowledge on the exact amount of labor time expended, organic fertilizer, and draft animals.[18]

Other researchers offered interesting case studies of HRS. Han showed that Jimo County in Shandong Province achieved remarkable development in the collective era, but after the implementation of decollectivization, mechanization decreased immediately (in some cases, peasants dismantled the tractors and divided the metal), and irrigation became a big problem as well.[19] Moreover, several other works showed that HRS had little impact on agricultural development. Bramall did a careful examination of county-level data in Sichuan Province, which was the model province of agrarian reform for quite some time. He found that those counties that were not decollectivized had no worse performance in agricultural production than those already decollectivized.[20] Moreover, after final implementation of HRS, those counties that adopted HRS did not have a surge in production; on the contrary, most of them experienced declines in production. Putterman also found that in Dahe County in Hebei Province, grain yields rose during the 1970s but stagnated during the transition period.[21] A detailed historical study of the Yangzi Delta highlighted the fact that decollectivization did not lead to productivity increase.[22]

As many empirical studies showed, the transition to HRS in certain localities did not necessarily lead to productivity growth; this evidence strengthens the suspicion about the role of decollectivization. But most of them did not provide a comprehensive examination of the nationwide transition, which is what this chapter tries to do below.

Replicating Justin Lin's Research

Lin is one of the most sophisticated researchers on the impact of HRS; his findings, published in the *American Economic Review*, show that almost half of the increase in output was due to HRS reform.[23] Lin was able to get detailed data for twenty-eight provinces and districts for the years 1970-1987, enabling him to form a panel data (repeated provincial observations over time), which is a much more fruitful approach than simply looking at the aggregated national production growth rate.[24] Using Lin's original dataset, we have replicated Lin's models in Appendix 1 and presented the main results in Table 3.4 (see page 50).

The most significant finding from Lin's models was the positive impact of HRS on the value of crop output. He went on to argue that from a growth accounting perspective, HRS could account for more than 40 percent of the productivity increase in agriculture.

However, it appeared that Lin's methodology was problematic in several ways. As Carolus argued, it might be overly simplistic to use a single theory and model to apply to nationwide data, given wide differences in institutions before decollectivization in each locality.

TABLE 3.4: Estimated Impacts of HRS

	Lin (1992) Replicated		Adjusted Models	
	[1]	[2]	[3]	[4]
HRS adoption (%)	.19	.15	.06	.06
(HRS)	(.03)	(.05)	(.05)	(.05)
Land	.65	.58	.69	.69
(Land)	(.06)	(.07)	(.07)	(.07)
Machine & animal power	.04	.10	.13	.13
(Power)	(.04)	(.04)	(.05)	(.05)
Labor	.14	.15	.13	.13
(Labor)	(.02)	(.03)	(.03)	(.03)
Fertilizer	.18	.17	.15	.15
(Fert)	(.02)	(.02)	(.02)	(.02)
Nongrain crops (%)	.67	.78	.85	.85
(Ngca)	(.23)	(.22)	(.23)	(.23)
Multiple cropping index	.20	.20	.25	.24
(MCI)	(.08)	(.08)	(.09)	(.09)
Market price/ input price at time t-1	.02			
(MPt-1)	(.05)			
Procurement price at time t	-.03			
(GPt)	(.02)			
Weather				.001
(W)				(.001)
Time trend (T)	Yes	No	No	No
Province dummies	Yes	Yes	Yes	Yes
Year dummies	No	Yes	Yes	Yes
Observations	476	476	420	420
R squared	87%	89%	89%	89%

Notes: Numbers in parentheses are standard errors; the coefficients of province dummies and year dummies are not reported. In all columns the dependent variables are log (value of output per team).

Agricultural Productivity and Decollectivization 51

Carolus also criticized the data on the labor force used in Lin's study: since the exact labor input in a crop sector is not available, treating the crop sector labor share in total rural labor and the output share in total agriculture output as the same might cause serious biases.

While acknowledging the problematic methodology involved in similar applied econometric work, we still try to focus on problems with Lin's approach. There are several key issues in Lin's empirical analysis. The first and most important is the incorrect use of the HRS adaption rate. As Lin explained, the HRS variable is the ratio of HRS adaption at the end of a given year. It is well known that agricultural production normally takes place intensively in certain seasons. So, if HRS adoption occurred after these seasons—for example,in late fall and winter—it was not likely to have any impact on productivity in that given year; it would only affect next year's production. Fortunately, there is some scattered evidence about the pace of decollectivization in China,which allows for some preliminary observations to be made. Table 3.5 (see below) presents some estimates from other scholars. It is clear that a big shift to HRS happened during the second half of 1981—from 11.3 percent in June to 38 percent in October. Another big jump in the HRS adaption rate took place between October 1981 and June 1982, but it is highly likely that a large portion of those changes happened at the end of 1981. A good case might be Heilongjiang Province, which was one of the most important grain-producing areas in China. The percentage of HRS in Heilongjiang was only 8.7 percent at May 1982; however, it quickly rose to 73 percent at February 1983.[25] Therefore, the usage of

TABLE 3.5: Pace of HRS Nationally

1980/01	1980/12	1981/06	1981/10	1982/06	1982/12	1983/12
0.02	5	11.3	38	67	70	94

Note: The numbers refer to the percentage of production teams that adopted HRS model.
Source: Wang and Zhou, 1985, 46; Bramall, 2000, 328.

end-of-year HRS will attribute a large part of production gains to HRS, while the credit actually belonged to other factors.

The second problem is that the construction of the price index does not fully capture the change in peasants' actual profitability and incentive change (as Table 3.3 shows). From 1981 to 1984 the index of above-quota prices relative to industrial input prices goes down, while in fact the profit margin went up. This could explain part of the reason why prices only had negligible roles in Lin's results, which is contrary to theory as well as common sense.

The third problem is that some important information—for example, weather changes—is not included. As previously discussed, the weather conditions were better during the transition period. It could be possible that this favorable weather change contributed to production. No such experiments were explicitly carried out in Lin's paper, although the two-way fixed-effect (controlling for province and time-specific factors) model might be able to capture the weather changes.

In light of these critiques, we have tested the role of HRS after adjusting for the timing of HRS as well as other problems. The main results are presented in columns 3 and 4 of Table 3.4. Appendix 1 presents some details of the methodology and models. The replications suggest that after using a one-year-lagged value of HRS, the strong impact of HRS completely disappears. The models also generate highly consistent estimates of other important coefficients compared to Lin's results.

According to the replications, the output changes seem to be determined mainly by the input usage changes along with changes in the cropping patterns, cropping intensity, and other year-specific factors like price adjustment and weather changes. The most important finding is that the HRS reform does not have any statistically significant impact on the output.

FURTHER DISCUSSION ON THE EMPIRICAL RESULTS

Although HRS did not have any significant impact on productivity directly, it could possibly have some unobservable influences on the usage of major inputs and therefore indirectly contributed to the output. Some discussions are presented below to address the concern.

Besides the input changes, other factors in the model were also likely to have contributed to the change in output. But these changed minimally during the transition period. For example, MCI decreased 0.3 percent during 1980–1984 (see Table 3.2). In addition, it is hard to single out their impacts; for example, the impacts of favorable weather are captured by the year dummies together with other possible year-specific factors like price changes. However, there are good reasons not to worry about these. First, weather and price changes were not due to HRS. Second, factors like declining MCI would not likely suggest any positive impact of HRS that we are trying to identify.

Therefore, what remains to be seen is whether the changes in the major four inputs—namely land, labor, power, and chemical fertilizer—were partly affected by the HRS reform.

First, the size of cultivated land began to decrease after the 1970s; it decreased by only 0.2 percent during 1975–1979, but then shrank by 1.5 percent during 1980–1984.[26] This occurred at the same time the MCI was declining, which means the size of total sown area decreased even more during the early 1980s.[27] Therefore, the changing land usage did not contribute to the dramatic output growth in the transition period. It is hard to find any positive role of HRS reform in the land input changes. However, it might be argued that HRS reform, which started nationwide in 1980, actually contributed to the accelerated decline of the cultivated land size—in other words, it dampened agricultural production.

Second, the total labor input in agriculture, as we discussed, is hard to measure given the fact that no specific data on labor force in the crop sector is available as well as the prevailing underemployment in the countryside. The coefficient of labor variable in the regression only gives us some crude evidence of the impact of the labor usage changes. If we adopt Lin's methodology of calculating the crop labor force as the total labor force in the agriculture sector times the value share of crop sector in the total agriculture output, the change in the crop sector labor force would be negligible, with the annual growth rate 0.5 percent between 1978 and 1980, and 0.9 percent between 1980 and 1984. If we look at the total labor force in agriculture as a proxy for the crop sector labor force, then the annual growth rate became 2.3 percent between 1978 and 1980, and 1.5 percent between 1980 and 1984.[28] Given the fact that the MCI was declining during the period, we might guess the actual labor input more or less stayed the same. Again, there is no clear link between the HRS reform in the early 1980s and the labor input changes.

Third, both machine power input and chemical fertilizer input changed considerably during the transition period and contributed greatly to the changes in output. But a closer look would reveal that both of them started to take off long before the HRS reform. As Table 3.2 shows, during the five-year period prior to HRS (1976–1980), machine power usage increased by 71 percent and chemical fertilizer usage increased by 118 percent. This dramatic increase continued in the 1980s; during the five-year period of HRS reform (1980–1984), machine power usage increased by 32 percent and chemical fertilizer usage increased by 37 percent. It is more than clear that China was experiencing rapid industrialization and the green revolution all through the 1970s and early 1980s, and the dramatic increase in machine power and fertilizer showed nothing more than the great achievements of the socialist period.

Finally, some special attention must be paid to the fertilizer factor, as it was also considered by Lin as the single most important input factor in output growth. There is literature pointing out that there are two main unobservable benefits with chemical fertilizer in China. First, the quality and quantity of fertilizer improved dramatically in the late 1970s because of large investments in the previous collective era. Second, the high-yield hybrid crops began to be introduced in the late 1970s (these had also been developed under the collective regime), which compounded the effects of fertilizer and the previously established water conservation.[29] Therefore, the huge impact of fertilizer from the regression exercise actually reflects the two important factors above.

Agricultural Productivity and Decollectivization

As previously noted, China's agriculture had always been severely fertilizer-constrained until the late 1970s when the prior chemical investments started to run properly.[30] It would be hard to argue that people increased their incentive to use fertilizer because of decollectivization; it simply became more available. From the demand side, the state made adjustments to the quota procurements in 1979, which increased the profit margins of the peasants, which might have contributed to their ability to purchase fertilizer.

It is hard to connect the HRS reform to any of these important input changes. Moreover, it is more than clear that the dramatic input changes in the transition period were indeed an endogenous result of the preexisting institutions: the remarkable development of the socialist economy in the former period built the conditions for the dramatic output growth. To sum up, there are very good reasons to conclude that the legacy from socialist agriculture, rather than the HRS reform, accounted for the most important part of the success is of the transition period.

4

The Political Economy of Decollectivization

INTRODUCTION

Decollectivization of China's rural economy in the early 1980s was one of the most significant aspects of the country's transition to a capitalist economy. Deng Xiaoping praised it as an "innovation," and its significance to the overall capitalist-oriented "reform" process surely cannot be overstated.[1] The Chinese government has repeatedly referred to the supposed economic benefits of decollectivization, claiming that it has "greatly increased the incentives to millions of peasants."[2] Nevertheless, the political-economic implications of decollectivization have always been highly ambiguous, and questionable at best. Individuals or small groups of peasants were frequently portrayed in mainstream accounts as political stars for initiating the process, but this served to obscure the substantial resistance to decollectivization in many locales. Moreover, the deeper causes and consequences of the agrarian reform are downplayed in most writings, leaving the impression that the rural reform was in the main politically neutral.

A few works did address the political economy of decollectivization, but even those often dealt in stereotypes and were highly consonant with the official history. One of the popular arguments was that peasants wanted freedom from collective controls, so they creatively and collectively dissolved their own collectives.[3] A typical analysis tended to follow this story line: collective farming caused years of poverty and laziness, so brave and wise peasants signed secret contracts to perform household farming. Due to the powerful incentive effects of decollectivization, agricultural production increased dramatically. Once decollectivization spread nationwide, with impressive results, the Chinese Communist Party had to accept this institutional innovation reflecting the will of the peasants.

However, as we have demonstrated in chapter 3, decollectivization did not have the acclaimed impacts on efficiency. This suggests that there were perhaps more important factors beyond the efficiency and incentive aspects offered by the conventional wisdom. In particular, a class analysis is missing from the mainstream stories.

This chapter explores the process of decollectivization from the perspective of political economy. I argue that decollectivization served as the political basis for the capitalist transition in China in that it not only disempowered the peasantry but also broke the peasant-worker alliance and thus greatly reduced potential resistance to the reform. The political significance of the rural reform for the CCP cannot be overstated, and this is exactly why the CCP interpreted decollectivization as spontaneous and purely economic.

DEBUNKING THE MYTHS AROUND DECOLLECTIVIZATION POLITICS

The two most prominent myths created regarding the history of decollectivization are these: (1) the whole movement was largely spontaneous and apolitical, and (2) the only people who opposed decollectivization were the cadre, not the peasants. Since these myths are the pillars of the mainstream interpretation, they are worth critical examination.

Spontaneous Movement?

Decollectivization in the 1980s has been labeled a spontaneous, grassroots collective action against the previous collectives. In this version of events, most peasants wanted decollectivization, and the CCP was passive in the reform. But a closer reading of the actual history reveals that the opposite is true.

All the anecdotes about peasants collectively dismantling their own collectives seem to be in conflict with the basic logic of decollectivization. The mainstream explanation for decollectivization was that peasants did not agree with collective production. But as Bramall argued, if the peasants could organize their decollectivization in the way they are said to have done, then collective agriculture would have been a huge success and there would be no need for decollectivization.[4] That is, there would have had to have been a history of collective organization for this to be possible. To be fair, this is not to deny there were singular cases of decollectivization in small groups; nevertheless it is simply ahistorical to explain the majority of cases in this way.

In fact, in the early days the CCP's own flagship journal, *Hongqi* (Red Flag) proudly claimed that decollectivization was carried out by local authorities following instructions from above.[5] We find more solid evidence of the coercive nature of the agrarian reform in the official provincial records. In 1980, the district of Shanghai, one of the most developed regions under socialist China, declared that it would not implement decollectivization. However, in 1982 it decided to follow the national policy and quickly decollectivized its rural economy.[6]

The district of Beijing also tried to maintain the collectives in the early 1980s. However, Hu Yaobang, then the national secretary of the CCP, criticized Beijing cadre for resisting decollectivization in 1982. After this the Beijing Communist Party Committee quickly made an announcement claiming that although some cadre had not freed their minds and still had reservations about decollectivization, the reform should nevertheless be implemented, and quickly.[7]

In Yunnan Province, only 3.5 percent of teams had been decollectivized as of March 1981. The provincial leadership held a meeting to "unify thoughts on decollectivization" in May and advocated a decollectivization model in November. By the end of the year, more than half the teams were decollectivized.[8]

In Zhejiang Province, the official record noted that local leaders were not enthusiastic about decollectivization and attributed that to "lack of awareness." Talk by provincial leaders on maintaining the collective economy was regarded as "inappropriate." These unusual tones suggest that there was fierce political struggle between the local leaders and the pro-decollectivization central leaders. In August and September, Zhejiang had several cadre meetings to correct "the leftist errors in the agrarian reform" and to advocate household farming. The result was clear: decollectivization rose from less than 40 percent in June 1982 to more than 90 percent by April 1983.[9]

Hunan Province had a similar story. Hunan leaders were initially supportive of the collectives. However, in the spring of 1981, several central leaders went to Hunan to push for decollectivization. After that the provincial party secretary had to officially apologize for his lack of understanding of the central policy and the slow pace of decollectivization. The local leaders then started the decollectivization campaign, and within one year nearly 80 percent of the teams were decollectivized.[10]

Du Runsheng, the architect of nationwide decollectivization, revealed more inside information in his recent memoirs. Du claimed that some provinces accepted household agriculture only after replacing their leadership; the list includes several important provinces: Fujian, Jilin, Hunan, Guangxi, and Heilongjiang.[11] Moreover, Du also documented how the central leaders used their authority to push the decollectivization campaign. For example, Hu Yaobang, the national leader of CCP, went to Hebei Province and criticized their slow adoption of the household agriculture system; the household model was rapidly implemented after that.[12] Hu also publicly declared that those cadres who opposed decollectivization should be removed.[13] Pressure from above was also well documented in the literature.[14] For example, one of the defenders of decollectivization admitted that "although family farming began as a peasant innovation, that did not mean all peasant communities wanted it." But he still claimed that after decollectivization most peasants appeared to accept their share of the land with pleasure.[15] Some authors are clearly selective in presenting evidence. Kate Xiao Zhou, for example, quotes from Shumin Huang's book *The Spiral Road* to show that collectivization was spontaneous; however, she ignores the story in the same book that suggests decollectivization was enforced by the CCP.[16]

It is difficult to say how many peasants actually favored family farming, but according to He Xuefeng, an expert on rural issues in China, at least a third of peasants in his national survey had considerable reservations about decollectivization.[17] It was clear that the CCP played a crucial role in the early 1980s as the whole reform was rapidly implemented nationwide.

Zhou claimed that no work team was ever sent down to the villages to carry out decollectivization. She regarded this as important evidence of the absence of state coercion in the decollectivization campaign.[18] But several provincial records mentioned large-scale work teams; for example, more than ten thousand people were sent down to implement decollectivization in Fujian Province.[19] Moreover, work teams may not have been necessary when the existing political machine was on board with decollectivation and politically capable. An interview about a team in Jiangxi Province vividly illustrates the passive role of the peasants.

> The Communist Party cadre had held a meeting at the commune. Then the team head returned and held a team cadre meeting. Cadre called the system "divide the land to the households" (*fen tian dao hu*). The cadre didn't propagandize the system; they just held a meeting [of team members] and said this was the way it was going to be done.[20]

Even researchers who were not necessarily supportive of the collectives claimed that the decollectivization campaign was far from spontaneous. Anita Chan, Richard Madsen, and Jonathan Unger document that, as with many previous campaigns, when Beijing indicated a decided enthusiasm to see decollectivization adopted, some local cadre who appeared reluctant to implement the reform found themselves publicly chastised for leftist thinking.[21] Thomas Bernstein admits that by 1982, adoption of the household model became a matter of compliance with the current party line and was pushed through regardless of local preferences.[22]

This evidence challenges the view that decollectivization was a spontaneous collective action and shows that the agrarian reform was highly political and led by the CCP from the beginning. This naturally leads to the question, what was the nature of the resistance to decollectivization in the early 1980s?

Opposition to Decollectivization

Let us turn to the second myth. There was significant opposition to decollectivization, and the mainstream concluded that this opposition must have come from some cadre who were simply afraid of losing control of peasants.[23] This is also summarized in a concise phrase often quoted in the mainstream media: "the top (leaders) agreed, the bottom (peasants) desired, the middle (cadre) blocked."[24]

Some cadre might not have wanted decollectivization because "management would become difficult," but it is hard to believe that a majority of cadre would simply oppose the policy from the central leaders because of fear of "losing control."[25] As we discussed in the previous section, opposing decollectivization was close to committing political suicide; on the other hand, following the central policy could be quite rewarding. David Zweig documents that the provincial party committee in Shaanxi Province changed the leadership in Zhidan County in 1978 because of its continued support for a radical agrarian policy (that is, collectivization).[26] In the winter of 1979 the new county leadership allocated land to groups and households in 90 percent of the teams in the county. This was not an isolated case. Dongping Han also noted that Jimo County in Shandong Province was forced to accept decollectivization and local leaders who opposed were removed from their office.[27] In an extreme case in Hebei Province, a rank-and-file pro-decollectivization researcher was directly promoted to the provincial standing committee of the CCP.[28] Provincial-level cadre resisted decollectivization for a short time, but as soon as they realized the intention of the central leaders, their attitudes "swung full circle" to secure their political positions.[29] There were still some pro-collective provincial leaders who were able to resist, but they could not continue supporting the collectives for very long.[30]

Roderick MacFarquhar observes that rural cadres were initially unhappy about their new tasks, but they soon realized that they could benefit from the reform by using political skills and connections to preserve their status and increase their incomes.[31] Interestingly, Shumin Huang also suggests that although ordinary peasants and workers in the collectives were very worried about their future and protested vigorously, many local cadre were enthusiastically promoting decollectivization because they could then take over the collective enterprises and make a profit.[32] The experience and connections they had gained as leaders of the collectives now allowed them to run what would now, in effect, be enterprises of their own. Dongping Han describes similar political changes.[33] With decollectivization, collective enterprises were left under the control of the village party leaders and managers, who often rented the enterprises or simply bought them outright despite strong resistance from villagers. Decollectivization disempowered peasants: the loss of collective economic interests fragmented their political power. Village leaders, in contrast, were able to concentrate political power in their own hands and thus gained the most from decollectivization.

Although we know anecdotally some high-level cadre also opposed the reform, their voices were never significant in the public arena.[34] Some authors tried to find some anti-decollectivization central leaders but their arguments were unconvincing. Take Kate Xiao Zhou for example: she identifies Prime Minister Zhao Ziyang as a central leader who opposed decollectivization in 1980, but on the same page she counts Zhao as one of the pro-decollectivization leaders on another occasion in the same year![35] In fact, the CCP's dominant figure, Deng Xiaoping, highly praised decollectivization as early as 1980, so it was very unlikely that any central leader would oppose it, a fact observed by MacFarquhar and confirmed by Zhao Ziyang himself.[36]

Huang documents a story in southeast China where the higher authorities and some villagers pressured the local leader to dismantle the collective, but the leader was able to resist until 1984.[37] He resisted not because he was afraid of losing control, since he would remain in a position of unchallenged power before or after decollectivization. He simply felt that a system that was working well should not be destroyed.

The official provincial records mention reactions from some peasants and cadres. For example, in Jilin Province, some old Communist Party members publicly claimed that there would not be any socialism without collectives, not to mention communism and a communist party. Some cadres burst into tears when they divided farmland and draft animals. They were sincerely afraid that the merits of collectives such as economies of scale, mechanization, and diversified production might get lost after decollectivization.[38]

Another report from Lu'an District in Anhui Province is also illuminating.[39] The author, Wang Yanhai, carefully documented two debates on decollectivization in 1979 among the cadre. The pro-collective cadre raised several major critiques of decollectivization. First, they observed that leadership, rather than decollectivization, explained the growth in agriculture. Second, only 30 percent of all the peasants who had more labor and human capital wanted decollectivization. Third, agriculture naturally required collective decision making in irrigation and farming. These were strong arguments, and not at all related to concerns about "losing control." So the pro-collective faction actually won the first debate. However, in the second debate, they were clearly under pressure from anti-collective leaders. As a result, they had to make significant compromises and their critiques were in fact dismissed.

The overall change to decollectivization was potentially beneficial to the cadre but not so much for ordinary peasants.[40] An award-winning novel, *Shan yue bu zhi xin li shi* (the innocent country moon) that was published in 1981 showed different attitudes on the reform in a very subtle way. A young, educated member of the cadre started decollectivization reform and other "leaders" opposed him while the "peasants" welcomed it; some anti-decollectivization women first opposed him but later agreed to his reform ideas.[41] In this novel, the contradictions previously mentioned were solved by the leader's superman spirit: he deliberately allocated inferior land to himself rather than take advantage of the land division. Moreover he worked day and night for free for those families with insufficient labor. However, the logical problem comes up again: if this leader was so charismatic and self-sacrificing, it is hard to imagine why he could not lead peasants in collective production.

The interpretation that depicts agrarian reform as a bottom-up movement originating with the peasants and opposed by local cadre is fatally flawed. The cadre and a small segment of the peasantry implemented and benefited from the reform. The average peasants were not enthusiastic about the proposed changes, and even opposed them in some cases. But if decollectivization was actually led by the CCP cadre and other advantaged groups, what was their primary goal? A brief review of CCP party lines on agrarian relations over the last three decades may shed some light on this question.

CHANGING POLITICAL WINDS

Mao's death in September 1976 marked a new era for China. Not long after, Deng Xiaoping became the most powerful person in the CCP Central Committee. Although he and his allies were longtime supporters of household production, it was not clear at the beginning that he wanted to dismantle the collective economy so rapidly. In his famous political speech in 1978, which outlined his plan for widespread market reforms, he only briefly mentioned agriculture.[42]

> Now the most important task is to increase the autonomy of factories and production teams.... How much wealth can be produced out of that!... The more wealth individuals create for the state, the more income they should receive and the collective welfare could be better.[43]

It was clear that he did not appreciate the Maoist collectives, with egalitarian income distribution. However, his critique of collective agriculture was very general. Around this time, the CCP also passed a new resolution on agricultural development, which encouraged collectives to rely on economic incentives and raised procurement prices to increase peasants' incomes.[44] Interestingly, the official CCP documents concluded that the main problem with collective agriculture was a legacy from "extreme leftists" in the Cultural Revolution. Nevertheless, all the new policies clearly retained the collective model.

In 1981, in an extremely important political resolution, the CCP finally reached a general consensus on the party's own history.[45] This report basically settled the debates within the party and provided a formal evaluation of Mao and his policies. It is interesting to note that although the report criticized many aspects of the Cultural Revolution and claimed it caused huge waste and unnecessary cost to the economy, it praised agriculture, with its increased grain production, as one of very few fields that had made "steady growth." Along this line, some history books also considered that agriculture was steadily growing in spite of the Cultural Revolution.[46]

But after the period of rapid decollectivization, the collective economy began to be seen as "stagnant." Hu Yaobang made this claim at the CCP's 12th National Congress in 1982: "[As we] corrected the previous 'left' error in the direction . . . agricultural performance was immediately changed significantly, from stagnant to prosperous."[47]

This became the standard description of collective agriculture from then on. The problem with collective agriculture was now not only identified with the extreme left, but with the normal left. At the same national congress, Du Runsheng, the head of the agricultural committee in the state council, explained clearly what the left error was: "The left error in agriculture had been there for more than twenty years until the responsibility system and especially *bao gan dao hu* [decollectivization] gave a strong fightback; long-suppressed incentives were released and long-lasting stagnation in agriculture was changed."[48]

So we see that the CCP began demonizing collectives at the 12th National Congress, only one year after the CCP praised collective agriculture for its "steady growth." However, the evaluation of decollectivization was also subject to change. After 1984, grain production stagnated for quite a while, and the CCP leaders changed their tune once again. Zhao Ziyang claimed agriculture needed policy support beyond decollectivization if it was to move forward.[49] Du Runsheng also downplayed decollectivization and said that agriculture ultimately depended on more technological progress.[50]

Interestingly, collective agriculture was not always demonized; in fact, the evaluation varied according to the political atmosphere. As D.Y. Hsu and P.Y. Ching discovered, Vice Premier Tian Jiyun once "acknowledged that the development of the agriculture infrastructure in the thirty years before the reform was the main reason for increases in agricultural production since the reform."[51] After the events in Tiananmen Square in 1989, political figures had to pretend to be a bit more "left" than they were in the 1980s. As Hsu and Ching observe, the leaders began repeatedly praising the achievements of the past forty years.[52] And in his speech at the 40th National Day celebration in 1989, Jiang Zemin, the new CCP national leader, deliberately changed the name of the agrarian reform from "household responsibility system" to "responsibility system."[53] This change, though subtle, implicitly understated the substance of decollectivization in the reform.[54] However, as the political pressure let up in the early 1990s, the name "household responsibility system" was restored and has remained since then. This was further confirmed by the report of the CCP's 15th Central Committee 3rd Plenary, in which the decollectivization of the rural economy was considered to have led, and greatly contributed to, the whole market reform.[55]

But since the new century began, the party line on household production has once again changed. Where the leaders once insisted that only individual or family farming could provide effective incentives, they now think incentives will be effective if farmworkers work together, as long as they are wage laborers working for a capitalist owner. The new political argument maintains the superiority of household over collective farming, but at the same time points out the limits of small household farming. As an alternative, it calls for land consolidation to reach a sufficient scale to launch agricultural investment and more efficient management. So household production is now considered inefficient. Of course, this assessment was never mentioned in the arguments against collective farming in the 1980s, when small peasants were declared the basis of agriculture modernization.[56]

The new line was clear in the resolutions passed at the CCP's 16th and 17th Central Committee in 2002 and 2008, respectively.[57] In particular, the Third Plenary resolution passed by the 17th Central Committee focused on rural development and encouraged peasants to transfer land use rights to concentrate land for more efficient, large-scale agricultural production.

The mainstream media has, for the most part, parroted the party line. At first, collective agriculture was good, but then the household model was applauded as the best. Now HRS is not productive enough and land consolidation is the answer. The ideal size of the agricultural unit has swung from large to small and then back to large. The ownership structure, however, has changed monotonically, with a continuous erosion of collective ownership. Perhaps these changes in party line can point us toward a causal explanation of the whole agrarian change. At least they make us more curious about the political motivation behind the push for decollectivization.

CAUSES AND CONDITIONS OF DECOLLECTIVIZATION IN THE POST-MAO CONTEXT

Although many members of the central leadership, including Deng Xiaoping, were favorably disposed toward household agriculture, this fact alone would not be sufficient to explain decollectivization of the whole rural economy. It is possible that the reform could have been enforced, but it would not have proceeded as smoothly as it did. It is also unlikely that Deng and other pragmatic bureaucrats would have supported something if the conditions were not right. This section analyzes the political causes of and, equally importantly, the conditions for decollectivization.

The "End" of Class Struggle

A short time after Mao's death, everything that sustained the Maoist society seemed to change. Indeed, the endless condemnation of the Cultural Revolution activists, the rapid restoration of the old cadre who had lost power during the Cultural Revolution and the previous political campaigns, and the emergence of so-called "scar literature" (*shanghen wenxue*) that described the destructive impacts of the previous era all marked Mao and his allies as political failures.[58] The bureaucrats reached out to form alliances with upper-level intellectuals who had lost their privileges during Mao's time. The new intellectual policies, such as reestablishing the national college entrance exam, were ways of gaining support from them. As Maurice Meisner argued, Deng Xiaoping succeeded in taking over power from Mao's immediate successor, Hua Guofeng, because of his wide support among the cadre, the military, and the intellectuals.[59] Although these political sectors may have differed in the past, and would differ again in the future, at the end of the 1970s they united under Deng on the need for a stable bureaucratic order and an end to Maoist mass movements such as the Cultural Revolution.

This change was reflected in the CCP's political and economic policies. The Third Plenary of the 11th Central Committee adopted a resolution stating that the central principle of the CCP was no longer "class struggle," but "modernization." The resolution also claimed that since the errors of the Cultural Revolution had been corrected, the main political enemy of workers and peasants was gone. This point was further developed in 1981, at the Sixth Plenary of the 11th Central Committee, where it was officially announced that class struggle was not the major contradiction in China anymore.[60] Of course, this assertion was true only in the sense that the bureaucrats and their allies now enjoyed overwhelming power over the country because their main political opponents inside the CCP had been defeated. However, the workers and peasants were yet to be tamed and remained potential enemies of the bureaucrats.

The strong push for modernization, plus the admiration of developed countries' wealth, created an ideology that China must catch up with advanced capitalism using their scientific and advanced technology and management. What was "scientific and advanced"? In fact, Deng already gave the answer back in 1978: the responsibility system. Specifically, this vague term meant more power to management, more power to technicians and intellectuals, and stricter labor discipline based on bonuses and punishments.[61]

In fact, starting in the late 1970s, capitalist-oriented reform was already being implemented in the urban industries.[62] And although the modernization that the CCP leaders meant was clearly different from socialism, and not likely to be welcomed by the workers, these tendencies and trends had not caused immediate social conflicts. This was largely because instead of trying to extract more from workers and peasants, the government pretended to compromise with them. In rural areas agricultural procurement prices were raised dramatically, and in urban areas workers got more dividends and awards.[63] These incentives were supposed to enhance the productivity of workers and peasants, and indeed agriculture and light industry enjoyed fast growth afterward. But the honeymoon between the capitalist-minded cadre and the workers and peasants soon came to an end.

Frustrating Urban Reform

The modernization program in industry was in fact a war on the workers in publicly owned enterprises. Jiang Zilong, then a worker writer, published a novel in 1979 that illustrates the conflicts between reformer cadres and workers.[64] In the novel, a newly appointed factory director and his wife—both very smart, both having recently studied management techniques in an advanced country, the Soviet Union—observe that, due to a loss of ideals after the Cultural Revolution, workers were lazy and shirking. Following the standard "scientific management" techniques, they used very harsh methods toward the workers, including firing more than a thousand non-tenured workers, in order to increase productivity. Many workers hated the new director and wrote complaints to the party secretary in the factory, hoping the CCP would save them. However, the party secretary was of the same mind as the director. In the end, leaders at a higher level encouraged the director to feel free to experiment, and the management in the factory decided to go to some advanced country to learn more about new management techniques.

What this novel described was exactly the direction of urban reform. Instead of increasing worker participation and political power, leaders became commanders and workers were merely disciplined to serve production. In this novel, the goal of the leadership was modernization, but that goal could easily change to profits for the leaders in the future because workers would have no power at all. Nevertheless, at the end of the 1970s, workers still had considerable power in most cases, and even many workers who supported reform did not accept capitalism. The author of this novel is typical: although he advocated for reform in the beginning, Jiang has rethought reform in recent years and publicly opposed the privatization and suppression of workers.[65]

According to MacFarquhar, urban reform posed great problems for the CCP since the opposition was very strong from the 1980s on.[66] Although it did not cause immediate social tension, the failure of urban reform was evident in the huge deficit of 1979–1980, which was caused not only by the increased pay for workers and peasants but also by large-scale imports from foreign countries under the ambitious modernization program.[67] The Chinese people were shocked by the resulting inflation, as there had been no inflation in Maoist China.[68] In order to balance the budget, the CCP had to close many factories and that caused massive unemployment.[69] As Wu Jinglian notes: "In the late 1980s, due to some negative effects of the New Great Leap Forward on state-owned enterprises, there were fiscal deficits, accelerating inflation, and chaotic economic order."[70]

Thus, it was clear that the compromise between cadre and worker was not going to continue. First, the basic idea of the reform was to discipline workers to make more profits, so sooner or later the conflict of interest would come to the surface. Second, even if the cadre planned to buy support for the reform from workers, they were not able to do so anymore, given the severe conditions in the cities.

The problems in the urban areas led to the first political and economic crisis of the post-Mao CCP. It became politically risky to proceed with the capitalist line since that would lead to direct confrontation with workers in bad economic conditions. So it was natural that the cadre turned to the rural economy in 1980.[71]

The Weak Link

The rural economy was indeed the Achilles' heel of the socialist economy. Not only were one-third of the collectives not in good shape, but also the more successful ones suffered from a number of problems.[72]

Collective agriculture had made impressive achievements. However, population growth due to better health care and other improvements in the quality of life canceled out much of the improvement. For example, in the commune that Sulamith and Jack Potter studied, per capita distribution (income from work points per person) fell from a high of about 180 yuan in 1962 to a level just over 100 yuan throughout most of the 1960s and 1970s, even though gross output kept increasing.[73] Although population growth began to slow down in the 1970s, it was not sufficient to overturn the trend. On the national level, grain production increased annually by 2.68 percent from 1956 to 1978; at the same time population grew annually by 1.95 percent, so there was limited improvement in per capita product despite the growth in agriculture.[74]

Second, there was a lack of mechanization in agriculture. Without sufficient mechanization and infrastructure, collective farming is not necessarily more productive than individual farming. In Mao's time, a lot of infrastructure was built by the communes; however, mechanization only started to increase rapidly in the mid-1970s.

Third, different historical paths led to different performances in collective farming. As William Hinton pointed out, the successful collectives he observed had a long history of land reform and military struggle against reactionaries. Many strong peasant political leaders developed through that process and led the collective production well.[75] In other places, such as Anhui Province, land reform and collectivization were quickly instituted by outsiders rather than by local political leaders. In those places, collective farming was never as widely accepted by the peasants.

Last but not least, the prevailing political stratification dampened the mobilization and organizational capacity of the collectives, which led to underperformance of collective farming. In other words, the lack of socialist superstructure (such as politics and power structure) reduced the peasants' potential support for maintaining the collectives in some cases. Chapter 5 will elaborate more on this point.

The underperformance of collective farming in many places made it an easier case for the central authority to stress the inefficiency of the collective regime and thus enforce the decollectivization reform. The political power of the peasants was never as strong as that of the urban proletariat, who had been through decades of experience with industrialization and political organizing. Therefore, the relative weakness of peasants both economically and politically made them the first major target after the failure of urban reform.

Selling Decollectivization

Even with a relatively less powerful peasantry, decollectivization was not easy. It faced opposition on all levels. The strong resistance was largely due to the benefits the peasants received from the collectives and longtime emphasis on collective farming during Mao's time. But the CCP was indeed able to convince many peasants that decollectivization would be both efficient and socialist. This campaign was so successful that it deserves a separate discussion. As a strange blend of bourgeois propaganda and old revolutionary slogans, the ideological campaign proved to be effective.

First, the leaders always tried to make it appear that the new policies were in line with the socialist tradition. From the very beginning, the cadres were very careful with their language. Take the term "responsibility system." It was deliberately vague—no one could reject the need for people to take responsibility for their work. In fact, during the Maoist period the collectives widely contracted out small jobs to either groups or individuals, but these measures did not change the nature of the collective.[76] However, radical decollectivization reforms were hidden under the name of "responsibility system" as if they were the same as the already existing small-job contracting under the collectives. The CCP also tried very hard to differentiate decollectivization from complete privatization by keeping nominal ownership of the land collective. This vagueness of propaganda helped peasants and cadres to interpret the reform as still socialist and progressive.[77]

An interesting anecdote illustrates the propaganda effect of the "responsibility" name tag. During the decollectivization campaign, Romanian government representatives visited China and asked whether the household responsibility system could be simply renamed "responsibility system" since the previous one looked too similar to privatization. This suggestion was quickly refused by the policy makers because they believed "household" (i.e., decollectivization) more than anything was the key to the reform package.[78]

We can observe the deliberate vagueness in two of the most popular terms of the decollectivization campaign. The first term, *da bao gan*, actually means "divide the land and work on your own." However, it has another possible meaning: "guarantee to work." Many people thought the term referred to the second meaning, which clearly does not have any political implication. The second term, *lianchan*, means "linking revenue to production," which means the collectives are not responsible for allocating income. But in Chinese, the term could also imply some sort of "cooperative production." Again, many people wrongly believed that it referred to the second meaning.

While the leadership failed to get workers' support for the reform, they succeeded with peasants. Through the transition period (1979–1984) peasants' income increased greatly mainly due to increased procurement prices. Propaganda attributed this achievement to decollectivization. Therefore, most peasants had a positive view of the rural reforms, at least at the beginning.

Finally, in face of challenges from the pro-collective camp, the reformers always avoided direct confrontation and used sophisticated diplomatic skills. For example, many pro-decollectivization reports in the early 1980s admitted that the rural reform could eventually lead to the dismantling of the collectives and the restoration of small peasant production.[79] However, they only acknowledged these problems at an abstract level; on a concrete level they would only present pro-decollectivization cases. They also argued that a small degree of decollectivization would not really hurt socialist agriculture. After all, they would conclude optimistically, with definitive support of further decollectivization as the "inevitable trend."

In summary, strong workers' opposition directly caused the failure of urban reform, which pushed the CCP to refocus its attention on rural reform. For all the factors considered above, rural collectives were vulnerable to attacks from the CCP. At the same time, we should never underestimate the importance of ideology in the nationwide agrarian reform.

POLITICAL CONSEQUENCES

With the success of decollectivization in rural areas, the CCP could restart their urban programs. This was clearly stated in 1984 at the Third Plenary of the 12th Central Committee.[80] Why was leadership so confident about dealing with workers now?

First, the peasants ceased to be an important political force in China. Decollectivization, which transformed the organized and collective peasantry into independent and competing petty producers, greatly disempowered the peasantry as a body.

The potential threat of peasant revolts was always immense to the CCP leaders, who had led the peasant revolution themselves. Even a decade after rural decollectivization, a Chinese vice premier reportedly claimed that no one in the present regime can hold onto power if there are problems in the countryside.[81] The leaders in the early 1990s knew that if the farms were recollectivized, it would inevitably lead to a severe deterioration in the relations between the peasantry and the party and government. The fear of an aroused peasantry also partly explained the leaders' unwillingness to set up a farmers' association despite numerous proposals.[82]

By disempowering the peasantry, the CCP successfully eliminated one big threat to the further transition to capitalism. For example, the peasants kept silent when political unrest caused by privatization and market reform accumulated in the late 1980s. When students in Tiananmen Square were asked where the peasants were, the answer was "They are all asleep."[83] At the same time, Deng Xiaoping assured other leaders that there was no problem with the peasants.[84] Even in riots that occurred in subsequent years, they were not as threatening as they could be if they were organized.

Second, the traditional peasant-worker alliance was broken. The temporary income increase in the countryside persuaded most peasants to support further reforms. There was also a long-run outcome: after agrarian reform the CCP encouraged individual peasants to sell their labor power in the city, providing an almost infinite labor supply to private industry in the urban areas. The urban labor glut greatly undermined the power of the old working class in publicly owned enterprises. It was under these conditions, including mass unemployment, that further capitalist-oriented urban reform was made possible.

The peasants were not any better off than urban workers, as their own political position declined and the need for the CCP to appease them decreased. Table 4.1 shows the changes of the ratio of urban-to-rural per capita income from 1980 to 2010. Although the peasants' passiveness in the late 1980s might be explained by their satisfaction that the urban-rural gap was dramatically reduced, the same logic cannot be applied to the later period, when the gap widened again after 1990. The decline of the peasants' political power also indirectly led to the relative decrease of state investment in agriculture. Clearly, the policy makers seemed to have forgotten the countryside. The share of rural expenditure in the whole fiscal budget declined from its high level in the collective era, even after adjusting for the declining rural population (Table 4.1, col. 2). Moreover, the rural

TABLE 4.1: Decline of the Countryside

	Urban-Rural Income Ratio		Adjusted Share of Fiscal Expenditure on Rural Areas (%)	Share of Infrastructure Building in Total Rural Expenditure (%)
1980	2.5	1971–1980	13.7	39.6
1990	2.2	1981–1990	11.8	22.7
2000	2.8	1991–2000	13.2	25.3
2010	3.1	2001–2006	12.8	25.0

Notes: Urban-rural income ratio is defined as the urban per capita disposable income divided by the counterpart in rural areas. The share of fiscal expenditure in rural areas is calculated as the share of per capita rural fiscal spending in national per capita fiscal spending to adjust for the changing population composition over time. The fiscal expenditure data after 2006 are not available owing to adjustments in the measurement.

Sources: Calculated based on Ministry of Agriculture, 2009; State Statistical Bureau, 2005, section 19, 30; State Statistical Bureau, 2012, sections 3.1, 9.2.

infrastructure expenditure share within the already small rural fiscal budget also went down dramatically compared to the collective era (Table 4.1, col. 3).

The workers and peasants were potential opponents of capitalism, and the CCP would have been unwise to face both at the same time. However, after dissolving the power of the peasantry, the CCP could now confront the workers alone. Even if the peasants began to experience hardship in later years, they did not have the solidarity and organization that they had enjoyed in the collective era.

The propaganda efforts of the CCP tried to make the rural reform look spontaneous and politically neutral. Yet it is also clear from the changing party lines that the reform was always a matter of politics. The rural reform served as the political basis for the later transition to capitalism, although the CCP always tried to hide this fact.

In fact, Mao made the politics of decollectivization clear as early as 1962: "Do we want socialism or capitalism? Do we want collectivization or decollectivization?"[85] In particular, he reminded everyone to "never forget class struggle." Although not many peasants and workers understood Mao's reminders at the time, they definitely understand them now.

―――― 5 ――――

The Achievement, Contradictions, and Demise of Rural Collectives

INTRODUCTION

Scholars critical of rural collectives often claim that because of flawed incentive structures or lack of supervision, the collectives suffered from inefficiency and work avoidance. These internal problems finally led to a bottom-up decollectivization movement in the early 1980s, which greatly increased agricultural productivity. But, as we have demonstrated, decollectivization was largely a top-down policy, and it did not significantly contribute to productivity improvement.

Those against collectives rightly point out that it was internal contradictions that led to the demise of the collectives, but they tend to overestimate the inefficiency issue. As a result, they exaggerate the positive aspects of decollectivization while downplaying its coercive nature. Their attempts to explain the problems of the collectives are not based on concrete empirics but are, rather, metaphysical, assuming certain features of human nature, like "laziness." At the same time, while many of those in the opposite camp are right to recognize the remarkable achievements of the collectives and the political economy of the decollectivization campaign, this strand of the literature still needs to explain the fact that decollectivization was instituted relatively peacefully and with little resistance from the peasantry.

This chapter contributes to the discussion by offering a case study of Songzi County, illustrating the arguments and evidence with both qualitative and quantitative data. Located in southwest Hubei Province, Songzi is close to the southern bank of the Yangtze River. Songzi has shared many of the key experiences of rural China: it was occupied by the People's Liberation Army in 1949, underwent land reform immediately afterward, and collectivization (as the whole country did) in the 1950s. Songzi also experienced the Great Leap Forward in 1958 and the "difficult" years after. The Cultural Revolution, which began in 1966, also shook Songzi for a while. In 1982, its local government followed the central policy and peacefully dismantled the rural collectives.

During the winter of 2010 and the spring of 2011, I conducted interviews with local peasants and cadres active in the collective era. I initially selected a few interviewees from recommendations from my local friends in the villages. I then talked to more people based on the first round of interviews. Appendix 2 provides some brief information about the interviewees. I consulted local official records such as *Xianzhi* (the county record) and *Shuilizhi* (the water conservation record). In addition, I also examined the collective accounting books, which contained information on the revenues, costs, and debts of the collectives.

In this chapter, I will show both sides of the rural collectives in Songzi: their remarkable achievements, as well as their problems with work avoidance and inefficiency, and the struggles during and after decollectivization. I argue that socialist economic organization naturally requires a socialist political process featuring democracy and participation. If the collectives are governed by stratification, it is likely that the peasants will carry resentment and demonstrate work avoidance. While the demise of the rural collectives was mostly due to political pressure from the Communist Party, the stratification contributed to peasants' passiveness and failure to resist the institutional change.

THE RURAL COLLECTIVES: INSTITUTIONS AND ACHIEVEMENTS

Beginning in the mid-1950s, peasants in Songzi were organized by the Communist Party cadres into collectives. Not all the peasants supported collectivization, but, unlike in some other parts of China, there was no major resistance recorded in the official history in this area.

In principle, the process of collectivization involved a series of steps: First, mutual aid teams were established in which peasants operated on their own. Then came elementary cooperatives, in which land and draft animals became collectively owned but peasants received income based on their labor efforts and dividends based on their land or draft animal contributions. Finally, advanced cooperatives were set up, dividends were discontinued, and members received income proportionate to their labor contributions only. The cadres also established people's communes to manage multiple advanced cooperatives. In practice, however, the process was very fast in some places, with some steps skipped, under the direction of the central and local leadership, particularly during the "socialist high tide" of 1955–1956 and the rush for communes in 1958.

In the early 1960s, the structure of rural society stabilized as a three-layer system: production team, brigade, and commune. The production team was the basic level of governance. Multiple production teams made up a brigade, and several brigades made up a commune. Although subject to orders from above, production teams were largely autonomous in production and distribution decision making, as described by the policy of "three-level ownership, team comes first" (*sanji suoyou, dui wei jichu*).

As the basic unit, a production team controlled most of its products and had an independent account separate from those of the brigade and commune. Normally, a team had some core cadres, including team head, production organizer, accountant, cashier, recorder (who recorded the work points), and women's organizer, as well as several other possible positions depending on specific conditions.[1] In theory, these positions were assigned in regular elections in which all members could vote. In practice, as my interviews showed, some teams did not hold a single election for more than twenty years, not because the peasants were not allowed to vote, but because they felt it unnecessary to vote again if the current leaders were doing a fine job or if they simply felt indifferent.[2] Brigades had a similar leadership structure, with the addition of a Communist Party secretary. However, instead of direct election by the members, the brigade's officials were elected by team-level cadres. At the level of the communes, which were approximately the size of towns, leaders were typically appointed by upper-level Communist Party officials.

The recorder of the production team recorded everyone's daily labor using a system of work points. Members of the collectives received their compensation based on their total work points during a production cycle (normally one year). In essence, an individual's work points indicated his or her share of the collective net revenue after subtracting taxes, fees, public reserves, and reproduction expenses. The work-point system varied across different areas, but in general it was a hybrid of both piece rates (based on work amount) and time rates (based on work time).[3] The collectives also assigned work points according to predefined labor grades or inherent capacity. For example, the work points for the best male laborer was set at 10 points per day and other people's work points were adjusted accordingly. The team leaders were also paid as a result of earning work points, but their tasks—such as attending political meetings—were hard to quantify in the work-point system. They were often assigned a higher number of work points than the average.[4]

This description merely offers a general picture; the actual institutions and norms differed significantly from one collective to another. More important for the purpose of this chapter is the question of how the collectives fared over the whole period. Based on historical data, the collectives contributed greatly to production and to the quality of peasant life. I will examine the achievements attained in four categories: agriculture, infrastructure, education, and health.

Agriculture

The major crops in Songzi include rice, cotton, and rapeseed (canola oil). During the collective era, there were frequent improvements in seeds and farming techniques. Songzi has a long history of rice farming, but it was not until 1955 that double-cropping rice was first tried. It took several years for the peasants to learn how to do double cropping, but by 1975 it was in use in 98 percent of all rice farms. In 1976, collectives started experimenting with hybrid rice and gradually adopted the technique.[5] Cotton growing in Songzi dates back more than six hundred years, and it was famous for its quality on the national market in the early twentieth century. The highest average yield recorded before 1949 was 247.5 kilograms per hectare in 1946. Only twenty years later, in 1966, the average yield exceeded 800 kilograms per hectare, and in the 1967–1979 period, there were five years when even this yield was exceeded.[6] Rapeseed saw two major seed improvements during the collective era, and the timing for sowing gradually shifted to enable multiple cropping.[7]

Table 5.1 (see page 85) presents the annual yields of the three major crops in Songzi from 1949 to 2005. Due to the lack of data in some earlier years, the yields are only reported for selected years. It may be misleading to directly compare the average annual growth rates between collective era and post-collective era because agricultural outputs in general fluctuate significantly across years and the yields in many years are not available. Nevertheless, we can still make some tentative observations based on the data.

Rice yields grew rapidly during the 1950s and then dropped dramatically following the Great Leap Forward period in the early 1960s. Yields recovered in the mid-1960s and the data show significant improvement in 1979. After decollectivization, rice yields continued to increase, albeit with several major drops in the late 1980s and 1990s. The growth of rice yields under collectives could be described as good rather than very impressive.[8]

For canola (rapeseed), the yield during collectivization was 517.5 kilograms per hectare. During the transition period, yields increased to 1,215 kilograms per hectare by 1982, but then stagnated for several years in the post-collective era. There was significant improvement in the early 1990s, but this was followed again by stagnation after the mid-1990s and a serious decline in the early 2000s.

For cotton, the story is more striking. Under the collectives the yields were clearly increasing, although it is hard to quantify the improvement owing to the poor quality of the data. On the other hand, cotton production clearly dropped after decollectivization and did not grow again until the 1990s. After reaching a peak in the mid-1990s, yields started to fall and stayed below 1,000 kilograms per hectare for several years. Yields started to recover in the 2000s, but the yield of 2005 (1,095 kg per ha) was still lower than that of 1984 (1,140 kg per ha).

As a whole, collective agriculture had impressive records. Yields grew significantly for all three crops, and two of them (cotton and canola) had better performance under the collective regime than in the later period. Thus it is fair to conclude that the collectives in Songzi achieved a good and sustained performance in agricultural production, although there was certainly room for improvement.

Infrastructure

Water management is perhaps the most important aspect of infrastructure for agricultural production and human welfare. Songzi is situated close to the Yangtze River and it has experienced numerous water-related disasters over the centuries. Between 1275 and 1911, sixty-one major disasters were recorded, most of which were floods and droughts. During the Republican era (1911–1949), there were twenty-two recorded disasters, including fourteen floods and eight droughts. Millions of people were affected; a single drought in 1941 affected more than 300,000 out of a total population of approximately 450,000.[9]

Although Songzi continued to suffer from natural disasters after 1949, the situation changed dramatically during the collective era. The collectives organized all available labor to participate in water

The Achievement, Contradictions, and Demise 85

TABLE 5.1: Crop Yields in Songzi County, 1949–2005 (kg per ha)

Year	Rice	Year	Canola	Year	Cotton
1949	2,685	1949	465	1949	210
1957	3,742.5	1955	517.5	1950–1957	285
1958	4,087.5	1960	652.5	1958–1962	450
1961	2,265	1971	817.5	1963–1979	675
1965	3,735	1978	735	1979–1983	495
1975	3,652.5	1982	1,215	1984–1985	1,140
1979	4,695				
1984	5,190				
1985	5,025	1985	1,275		
1986	5,475	1986	1,125	1986	1,110
1987	4,620	1987	1,155	1987	990
1988	5,547	1988	1,200	1988	930
1989	5,465	1989	1,275	1989	705
1990	5,760	1990	1,395	1990	1,245.00
1991	5,608	1991	1,605	1991	1,200.00
1992	5,971	1992	1,545	1992	1,560.00
1993	6,027	1993	1,755	1993	1,230.00
1994	6,519	1994	1,815	1994	1,230.00
1995	6,390	1995	1,800	1995	1,515.00
1996	5,760	1996	1,740	1996	1,155.00
1997	6,645	1997	1,800	1997	1,455.00
1998	6,600	1998	1,725	1998	600
1999	6,765	1999	1,650	1999	780
2000	6,780	2000	1,740	2000	870
2001	6,780	2001	1,635	2001	1,245
2002	7,005	2002	1,320	2002	1,200
2003	6,585	2003	1,440	2003	1,050
2004	6,735	2004	1,830	2004	1,037
2005	6,757	2005	1,756	2005	1,095

Sources: Songzi Shizhi Committee, 2011, Tables 9.1.68, 9.2.69, 9.3.70; Songzi Xianzhi Committee, 1986, 288, 292, 294.

management construction. In a relatively short time, a system of drainage, dams, and reservoirs was established. Among these, Weishui Reservoir deserves special mention. Like many reservoirs, the project started in 1958 during the Great Leap Forward. Tens of thousands of peasants contributed to the project, which took twelve years of manual labor to finish. The dam itself is nearly 10 kilometers long—one of the longest man-made earth dams in Asia. One can get a sense of the power of the rural collectives from this huge project.

Table 5.2 (see below) provides some statistics on infrastructure building in Songzi from 1956 to 2010, focusing on reservoirs and culverts. It is clear that most of the infrastructure was built in the collective era. One reservoir was built in the 1981–1990 period, but even that project started in 1974. Similarly, the two culvert constructions after 1991 were actually projects to rebuild old culverts that had been constructed before 1980. Infrastructure construction basically stopped after decollectivization. It is therefore justified to claim that the rural collective provided the crucial agricultural infrastructure that has remained important.

Education

Education was, and is, largely a privilege in Songzi. By the spring of 1949, only 20 percent of school-age children were enrolled in primary

TABLE 5.2: Water Conservancy Projects in Songzi, 1956–2010

	Reservoir		Culvert	
	Number	Irrigation	Number	Irrigation
1956–1970	7	24,727	3	7,733
1971–1980	6	2,167	5	3,500
1981–1990	1	333	2	266
1991–2010	0	0	2	6,466

Note: The years in the table refers to the completion date of the projects. The actual starting dates were often five to ten years before completion. Irrigation (in hectares) refers to the total effective irrigation size under the projects during that decade.
Source: Songzi Water Bureau, 2008, 91, 121.

schools.[10] For peasants and other working families, middle school and high school were luxuries. By 1949, there were only three middle and high schools, in the urban areas of Songzi, with a total of approximately 1,400 students.[11]

The rural collectives achieved a fundamental change in the accessibility of education. In 1956, there were nineteen rural primary schools, with 1,822 students, and a further seventy-seven urban primary schools. In 1960, the collectives had established 389 rural primary schools, with 31,599 students.[12] Nearly every brigade had a primary school. The collectives also started to build part-time primary schools and work-study primary schools in order to give busy peasants some basic education. The total number of primary schools (full-time and other types) increased to 1,327 in 1965; with a rate of enrollment for school-age children of more than 90 percent.[13] In the 1970s, most communes set up their own high schools; every brigade had a middle school and a primary school, and some of the rich brigades even had high schools.[14] The teachers and staff members were considered workers under the communes, and they got work points like any other peasant in order to receive a share of their collective's net revenues.

Table 5.3 (see page 88) gives a glimpse of the achievements mentioned above; school enrollment at all levels increased dramatically during the collective era. It is interesting to note that school enrollment reached its height in the late 1970s but then started to decrease significantly, especially for high school. During the Cultural Revolution, rural collectives began to set up their own schools to offer education to the children. This trend continued until 1978, when the government deemed the rural middle and high schools to be of low quality and shut them down.[15] After decollectivization, rural collectives simply ceased to exist and were thus no longer able to support local education.

It is, of course, true that most of the education offered in the rural schools was not as good as in the resource-rich urban key schools. For example, it was simply impossible to find enough experienced high school teachers when enrollment increased tenfold. It was standard

TABLE 5.3: Formal Education in Songzi

	Enrollment			Staff	
	Primary	Middle	High	Primary	Other
1949–1955	18,829	854		709	41
1956–1960	63,262	3,678	482	1,804	104
1961–1965	74,627	3,003	461	2,269	154
1966–1970	88,918	6,052	442	2,881	534
1971–1975	119,941	22,883	5,313	4,469	1,694
1976–1978	134,489	47,363	16,195	4,923	3,743
1979–1982	121,732	39,566	8,059	4,643	3,326
1983–1985	117,859	41,436	4,930	4,944	2,315

Notes: Enrollment refers to the annual average enrollment in primary, middle, and high schools during the given period. Staff refers to the number of teachers and staff in primary and middle or high schools,

Source: Songzi Xianzhi Committee, 1986, 557, 565.

practice for the collectives to ask newly graduated high school students to teach middle school—the best they could offer, given their level of development. Nevertheless, the rural collectives did provide the institutional foundation for basic education for every school-age child. Concerns about quality should have led to rural schools being improved over time, not shut down. Closing rural schools restricted access to education to just a small portion of the population, mostly urban.[16]

Health

Progress in public health during the collective era was impressive. In 1947, life expectancy in Songzi was 28.3 years; by 1979, life expectancy had reached 59.73 years.[17] The mortality rate dropped from 1.04 percent to 0.71 percent between 1957 and 1985; and by the 1979–1982 period, the mortality rate for children under the age of fifteen had dropped to as low as 0.34 percent.[18] Behind these changes was the establishment of a rural health care system during the collective era.

Beginning in 1958, every commune got its own small hospital, and starting in 1959, every brigade established its own health station.

TABLE 5.4 Medical Institutions in Songzi, 1950–1985

Year	Institution	Staff	Bed
1950	1	232	8
1956	28	765	272
1966	148	1,058	280
1970	128	1,481	417
1978	82	2,222	1,616
1980	81	2,419	1,772
1982	86	2,518	1,708
1985	127	2,761	2,110

Source: Songzi Xianzhi Committee, 1986, 668.

Moreover, the rural collectives developed their own cooperative medical care. In this system, each peasant in the collective (commune or brigade level) contributed a fixed fee per year, and the accumulated funds covered all kinds of the local health stations' expenses, including equipment, medicines, and payroll. If the expenses exceeded the deposited fees, the collectives would cover the deficits from their surpluses. It was this cooperative system that made health care accessible and affordable to peasants; without the rural collectives these improvements would have been unimaginable.

The rapid development in health care can also be seen in the number of beds and the number of staff in the medical care system. Table 5.4 (see above) presents figures for the number of medical institutions, staff members, and beds in selected years during the collective era. Although the data do not include the village level health stations, they do include the commune hospitals and give us a broad sense of the expansion of health care in this period.

THE CONTRADICTIONS WITHIN THE RURAL COLLECTIVES

Having sketched some of the achievements of the rural collectives, we will now focus on their internal contradictions. We do this by examining two persistent issues: the absence of a socialist political process, which led to widespread social and political stratification (and work avoidance) within the collectives; and the relatively low quality of life in the collectives. Both aspects presented serious challenges to the collectives and contributed to their eventual peaceful demise.

One of the greatest historical tragedies in the People's Republic of China was the severe famine during the late 1950s and early 1960s. Songzi did not escape: the crude mortality rate increased from about 10 percent in 1957 to nearly 37 percent in 1960, dropping back to the 10 percent level in 1961.[19] The great famine represents a crucial historical lesson for rural development. The collective regime at the time was at least partly responsible for it, but many of the famine-related problems of the collectives were short-lived.[20] This book therefore views the great famine as a shock to the collectives but not as one of the persistent problems that we are trying to identify. For instance, the fact that the production teams lost their autonomy to the communes and counties during the famine definitely contributed to the excessive grain procurement and other destructive practices in the countryside at the time. But this structural distortion was later corrected as production teams largely regained their autonomy in 1961. Collective food production dropped significantly during the 1959–1961 period, but it then increased again, and no further systemic food shortages occurred.

Stratification, Work Avoidance, and Efficiency

One of the most misleading discussions on the rural collectives is the issue of work avoidance. In the conventional wisdom, work avoidance was caused by egalitarianism. Deng Xiaoping once famously said that egalitarianism actually led to general poverty.[21] Some writers considered the rural collectives to have been too egalitarian, which caused inefficiency and brought about the demise of the system.[22] Some studies claimed that due to the high monitoring costs, the peasants shirked as much as possible, and this led to inefficiency.[23] This view is consistent with the assumption that human nature is indolent, self-centered, gullible, and responsibility-averse.[24] I would argue that we need to keep in mind the impressive records of the collectives, especially compared to the post-collective era. There was certainly work avoidance in the collectives, but I will argue that this was not the result of egalitarianism or the collective regime per se, but rather the by-product of nonsocialist superstructure (such as politics and power structure), including stratification.

The major material incentive structure in the collectives was the work-point system, which functioned fairly well. Every team had a recorder who assigned different work points according to labor undertaken, and the work points would finally translate into income distribution. Unlike the homogeneous and rigid institution that exists in the popular imagination, peasants in the rural collectives developed differing rules according to local conditions.[25]

Peasants were very resourceful in establishing the collective institutions. In general, the principle of "allocation to labor" was maintained. Two common incentive structures ensured intense effort and a fair distribution of rewards. In agriculture, the toughest and most important jobs are sowing and harvesting. Every team kept a complete and detailed record of the team land, in which the characteristics and the size of each plot were clearly measured. Every plot in the village had a nickname that was known to everyone, such as First-Hill Plot, Second-Ditch Plot, Knife-Handle Plot, etc. On the eve of harvesting, the peasants would evaluate the output from each plot and draft a work-point assignment guideline. If the crops grew high in the plot, which meant that manual labor would be somewhat easier, the proposed work-point assignment would be relatively lower; if the crops grew very dense, the proposed work-point assignment would be higher. This seemingly subtle task can be handled very well by any experienced peasant, just as college professors are capable of grading students and writing papers. The process was open to criticism and bargaining: if no one agreed to harvest a plot for the proposed number of work points, for instance, the cadres would have to change the work-point assignment until people were willing to take on the job. After this process, every specific plot was assigned to a laborer. Monitoring was not necessary. Everyone simply came to the recorder, reported which plots he or she had finished, and got the proposed work points. It was not possible to get a free ride, since everyone knew who was working on which plot and how hard he or she had worked.[26]

In other circumstances, like construction projects, the peasants also developed ways to make sure the work was done properly. One common method was to form work pairs, meaning that two people had to agree to work together. In a team where everyone knew each other through the collective labor process, people would only choose to work with the hardworking, honest people. Those with bad reputations would have a very hard time finding partners other than from among other workers who also had bad reputations. Under this type of system, the free-rider problem was minimized.

The work-point system per se was well developed and in general it allocated income properly. Many peasants would claim that they worked day and night during the collective era; indeed, most villages only had five days of vacation per year during the spring festival, whereas nowadays they have much more leisure time.[27] So where and when did work avoidance happen? In order to answer this question, two kinds of work avoidance need to be distinguished. First, in any collective there could be people who did not like working and tried to minimize their efforts: such shirkers were not a majority, but they weren't altogether uncommon. Huaiyin Li comments that "covert and minor slacking occurred, but flagrant shirking was unlikely to prevail where the villagers were subject to informal and formal constraints."[28] Second, there were cases, usually in the poor collectives, in which the whole team simply did not function well as a unit and everything seemed to be in a mess. This second form of work avoidance took place where the "informal and formal constraints" did not work.

The first form of work avoidance describes a personal characteristic—like laziness—and it was not a major concern of the peasants as long as it did not cause unfair income distribution in the collectives. As mentioned above, the work-point system worked well in most cases, and it was hard for people to take advantage of the system.

Sometimes people got paid more than they deserved; these cases were normally the result of cadres abusing their authority: the overpaid workers were either cadres or closely connected to them. In short, this was a result of the political stratification within the system.[29]

The second form of work avoidance was severe and deserves more attention. Productivity could vary widely across brigades within the same commune or across teams within the same brigade. Those low-performing, usually poor collectives were often described as "lazy," but the more accurate label might be "dysfunctional."

Similar phenomena have been documented elsewhere. The Communist Party of the Soviet Union made this observation in the 1930s: "It often happened that slackers received higher return than conscientious hard-working collective farmers. These defects in the management of collective farms lowered the incentive of their members."[30] Mao also said that if there was a clear difference between cadres and workers, "workers will not consider the factory as their own. The bureaucratic attitude of cadres will make workers unwilling to stick to the labor disciplines and the bureaucrat lords are always the first to break the rules."[31]

A local cadre told of his experiences working in such a situation. In 1979, he was sent by the county government to an extremely poor team. The peasants there had one meal per day in the low season, two meals per day in the busy time; the whole brigade could be characterized as depressed and dysfunctional. The leaders were particularly bad: the party secretary of the brigade had improper sexual relationships with several women, and the team head also tried to take advantage of a newly "sent-down" female student by commanding her to stay in his house. The cadre's story continued:

> I decided to take over the political leadership of the team and started to do everything as a team head. I held organizing meetings to plan the whole year's production, and on the next day, I was the first one to go to the fields to work, and I continued doing that thereafter. Besides working, I lived the same life as everyone did; it was called "same food, same house, and same

work." After a few days, the peasants began to work with me and they worked really hard. The whole depressing atmosphere was replaced with an energetic and colorful environment. In that year, the team's output doubled without any increase in material inputs.[32]

This story clearly suggests that "laziness" might be changed with a different political environment.

When Carl Riskin discussed the issue of work incentives in the Chinese collectives, he argued that the Maoist system (payment according to merit, collective material incentives, participatory management) had significantly motivated peasants' dedication to their work.[33] This positive attitude toward work, or X-efficiency, explained the creativity and effort under the collective regime. However, it is also clear that if the system did not work, the negative attitude toward work could significantly decrease the effort. If the cadres were corrupt and did not work with the peasants, for instance, the latter would simply consider themselves to be low-paid employees and become easily demoralized. However, if the cadres were hardworking and honest, people would regard the collective as their own and keep up morale and work effort.[34] In fact, the peasants repeatedly emphasized the role of the cadres and political leadership in the interviews. A former team head explained the key to running a successful team: "First, do not be selfish; second, take the lead in all kinds of work."[35]

In essence, then, the work avoidance problem is the story of conflict between socialist economic base and nonsocialist superstructure. In the socialist collectives, the means of production were publicly owned and people worked for the whole community, not for themselves individually. Such socialist economic organization naturally requires a socialist political process that featured democracy and participation. If this condition is not fulfilled, it is likely that the peasants will build up resentment and demonstrate work avoidance.

In practice, neither stratification nor work avoidance necessarily led to inefficiency. Stratification, although detrimental for a socialist collective, is a basic element of class society. A highly exploitative capitalist firm can still be efficient if there is sufficient supervision. Similarly, a collective with clear stratification and work avoidance could still be productive, given enough supervision. On the other hand, a democratic and egalitarian collective may not be so efficient if the leaders are inexperienced and not good at organizing. Sometimes the peasants described their leaders as "good fellows" (*lao hao ren*), which meant they were socialist-minded but not good organizers.[36] In a nutshell, it was the lack of socialist political process, rather than the opposite, that contributed to the unsatisfactory performance of some collectives. Although it may be convenient to explain this as laziness in casual speech, the discussions of work avoidance are largely misleading.

The Persistence of Political Stratification

Many peasants identified political stratification within the collectives as a major problem.[37] But how did the nonsocialist superstructure persist? The political system in the collectives was formally democratic; as Sulamith Potter and Jack Potter commented, government at the team level was democratically chosen.[38] But history repeatedly warns us that appearances can be deceiving. That is, democracy should not be taken at face value.

There were several historical reasons why the rural collectives were not so democratic in practice. First, many peasants were illiterate and had little experience of self-management. Second, the prestige enjoyed by many rural cadres because of their contributions to the revolution and their years of hard work meant that they expected their orders to be readily obeyed rather than questioned. Third, although team leaders were chosen by members, the upper-level cadres in brigades and communes, who had much more power, were not elected by the peasants and had much less direct connection to the peasants.

However, none of this implies that the cadres had comparable power to the landlords before the revolution. As Huaiyin Li has pointed out, cadres in the collectives faced severe political constraints compared to their counterparts in both the prerevolutionary and post-collective periods.[39] Moreover, many cadres in the collective era were very self-disciplined, particularly relative to the cadres nowadays. However, even the subtlest barrier to democracy may lead to stratification. As the leaders of the collectives, the cadres were in charge of organizing production and distribution, a process that continuously reproduced stratification. That stratification was most starkly apparent in work organization and in sexual relationships.

Although it was not easy for the cadres to take advantage of their position to reward themselves with money, they had the chance to use their power to escape from manual labor or punish peasants by assigning tough work to them. When the team cadres went to meetings or simply hung around the fields, they still claimed to be working; this caused tensions between peasants and cadres. For example, in Xiliu Village, a team head did not participate in the work but claimed he had done a lot. Instead of assigning a work-point number, the recorder ironically wrote down: "He flew to the west, then to the east, doing nothing."[40] Also, assignments with different levels of difficulty were sometimes awarded the same work points, so the cadres could assign tough work to those whom they did not like, a practice that was not uncommon, according to my interviewees. In some stories, people tried to bribe the cadres to get better job assignments and "more consideration" on other things, including but not limited to letters of recommendation for urban and military jobs.

Rewards for the cadres also took the form of sexual relationships. In the early spring of 1983, the sudden death of a female peasant in Xiliu Village became the talk of the day for people in Songzi County. Yang Chuanrong's body was found in a small pond. The police soon announced that Yang's death was an accident, not a murder. This statement was welcomed by village leaders, including Yang's husband, Zhou Xianyin, who was party secretary for the village. The announcement was met with fierce opposition from peasants, however. The police were forced to carry out another investigation, but they arrived at the same conclusion. The protest continued until the fourth investigation, when police officers finally concluded that it was Zhou himself who had ordered another peasant to kill his wife. Zhou had long been planning the murder so that he could marry another village woman who had been his mistress for seven years.[41] Zhou was sentenced to death soon afterward. He was not a mob boss: indeed, he had been considered a model cadre of rural collectives for years. But he was so powerful that he and his allies managed to manipulate the investigation results three times. It is clear the cadre-peasant relationship was not in harmony.

The manifestation of stratification via sexual relationships was clearly not limited to Songzi. William Hinton noted in his classic book, *Fanshen*, that in 1948 corrupt cadres abused their power in order to have improper affairs with village women.[42] Similar stories emerged twenty years later when Hinton revisited Longbow Village.[43] The basis for these inappropriate relationships is clear. The male cadre were able to have mistresses because of their influence on the local economy and politics. They could use their power over job assignments and loans to indebted households to extract sexual favors from village women. Starting from the 1960s, urban students were "sent down" from their schools to villages to get some experience in rural manual work. In order to go back to town to continue studying, they needed recommendation letters from the rural cadres, which created additional opportunities for abuse by the cadres.

There were historical conditions underlying these problems that could not be easily changed. For instance, during the socialist education movement in the early 1960s, an outside supervision group found Fan, a brigade-level party secretary in a nearby county, to be a problem: Fan collected bribes from every team, escaped from manual labor as much as possible, and showed favoritism in distribution decisions. The supervision group believed that Fan should be replaced. But Fan warned them that the brigade could not function without him. The work group had an emergency meeting, evaluated the situation, and made a new decision: Fan would stay in his position until another suitable leader was found. Although Fan was demoted for a short while, he returned to his original position after one year. According to someone on the work team whom I interviewed, Fan was one of the few educated people in that village; he was also a strong leader and a great speaker, so it was nearly impossible to find an alternative within the village.[44]

Another story originated in a nearby county, but it helps to illustrate the general picture. One day in the early 1960s, a brigade head suddenly asked a male peasant to go to work on a construction project outside the village; the peasant duly packed and started his journey. Before he left, his wife asked him several times to stay at home, but she failed to persuade him. On his way, he kept thinking about his wife's strange behavior and finally decided to go back to check if she was alright. When he got back, he discovered that the door of his house was locked from the inside. He got into the house through a back window and found the brigade head and his wife on the bed. The angry peasants of that brigade arrested the brigade head and sent him to the commune level to be punished. However, the commune leaders just rebuked the brigade head and sent him back to his original position. The explanation from the commune leaders was that this person was the only one capable of managing production in the brigade, so dismissing him would cause serious problems in achieving production goals.[45]

During the Cultural Revolution, massive political struggles became possible. Political stratification was challenged but not effectively changed.[46] Yang was a team head for twenty years from the 1950s to the 1970s, and during the Cultural Revolution his opponents criticized him for his bad temper toward the masses. He stepped down twice because of this opposition, but both times he was asked to return to office within three months. No one else had as much experience in organizing production; his opponents simply could not get the ball rolling after taking office. On another occasion, commune leaders were required to attend a meeting during which the masses could criticize the leaders freely. The meeting was two days long, and the leaders had to keep standing from dawn to evening. However, after all the harsh criticisms, the leader of the opponents came to the stage and announced proudly: now that the revolutionary meeting is over, let those in power (the old leaders) remain in charge of normal business![47]

The Achievement, Contradictions, and Demise

Dongping Han noted that the Cultural Revolution significantly empowered the peasants in his hometown.[48] But this might not have been the general case. There were indeed struggles against stratification, but the status quo was not significantly changed. Sustaining democracy would have required more fundamental changes than can be accomplished in a few years.

Pro-accumulation Policy

Many peasants felt that the quality of life under the collectives was poor.[49] This comment contains a grain of truth, especially in comparison to the material life of ordinary peasants nowadays. We are not talking about modern consumer goods but about a low level of basic subsistence, for example, meat and rice consumption per year. There are no detailed data on personal consumption in the Songzi countryside, but the national figures suggest an overall sluggish improvement: annual per capita rural grain consumption increased slightly from about 186 kilograms in 1955 to 193 kilograms in 1978, while the consumption of pork grew from 4.19 kilograms to 6.37 kilograms and edible oil dropped from 1.72 kilograms to 1.05 kilograms.[50]

The poverty was mainly caused by two factors. The first was that the increase in production (especially of food) was largely offset by the increase in population. For example, in 1949, Songzi's total grain output was 134,160 tons, while total population was 490,827; by 1979, the total grain output had increased to 308,640 tons (a 130 percent rise), but the population had also increased, to 813,824.[51] The grain availability per capita increased from 273.5 kilograms to 379 kilograms, an improvement of nearly 40 percent over thirty years. While impressive, this still left peasants poor in absolute terms, since the starting point in 1949 was on the edge of starvation.

Although population increase slowed down the improvement in per capita consumption, this increase needs to be put into perspective. Between 1928 and 1949, Songzi's population increased by only 0.4 percent, or approximately 2,000 additional people.[52] Extreme poverty, never-ending wars, and natural disasters all contributed to the slow population growth. After 1949, as the rural collectives began to cover health care and basic needs, and with the tragic exception of the great famine, population grew steadily.

The second major factor was the state policy that favored rapid industrialization. Two aspects of this pro-accumulation policy are directly connected to the slow improvement in peasant consumption levels: labor accumulations and personal debt.

The first aspect involved the Maoist labor accumulation schemes, which made a significant contribution to the growth of agricultural productivity and rural development in general.[53] They represented a low-cost and efficient means of accumulation and had long-lasting positive impacts on the people of Songzi, especially relative to the financial constraints experienced in other developing countries, such as India.[54] Songzi, like many other places in China, underwent a huge amount of self-financed infrastructure building during the collective era. The labor for these projects often came from the local rural collectives; according to my interviews, average labor time for a normal peasant on these outside projects was one month per year. The only compensation provided by the county government was food, which was procured from the rural collectives. The laborers could also get work points for the construction work, which counted toward their share of the collective output at the end of the year. But since the construction work often did not immediately increase the output of the collectives, this mechanism effectively required the rural collectives to subsidize the projects and did not always bring the expected improvements in quality of life.

The second aspect is the widespread phenomenon of indebtedness in the collectives. In fact, in interviews and other historical accounts, "debts to the collectives" was a recurring theme. Some families in rural collectives were never out of debt, no matter how hard they worked.[55] In news reports and pro-decollectivization novels, the story often went like this: there was an extremely poor team where every family was in debt, but after dividing their land, within one or two years they were free of debt! Although most of the team-level accounts from the collective era were discarded after decollectivization, some local cadres still kept records at home. The records that we analyze here are from a team in the Yongjiu brigade in Babao Commune in 1981, just before decollectivization.

The team comprised sixty-three households, two-thirds of whom were in debt to the team in 1980. After one whole year's work, more than half of them were still in debt. According to interviews, this team's debt problem was certainly not the worst in the commune. The (accumulated) average debt per household at the end of 1981 was 720 yuan; the average allocation per household for the year 1981 was just 615 yuan. Thus, a whole year's work was not enough to pay off the average household debt.

A closer look at the household data reveals that the burden of debt was not shared equally. Those indebted in 1980 were likely to be in debt again the next year and those without debt were also likely to be free of debt in 1981. The persistence of debt can be seen in Figure 5.1 (below), which plots the final debt from 1981 against the final debt from 1980. Although the absolute number of indebted households

FIGURE 5.1: Household Debt

decreased from forty-one to thirty-three in 1981, the effective debts per household (total debts divided by the number of indebted) actually increased from 265 yuan to 416 yuan (a 57 percent increase). Meanwhile, the effective allocation per household was 225 yuan; the gap between better-off families and poor families could thus be huge. This analysis reveals that a portion of the team was mired in debt. It also implies that the collectives were not as egalitarian as is often claimed. This confirms the suspicion that there may have been large differences between families within any one team.[56]

Where did these debts come from? During the year, peasants labored to get work points. At the end of the year, the collective calculated the revenue from its products (agricultural and industrial), and after deducting production costs and all kinds of accumulation, the rest was distributed in proportion to the work points each laborer had accrued during the year. There were also pre-allocations to distribute food rations to households during the year. Peasants sometimes also needed cash, so they borrowed from the collectives. Once the peasants received their allocation from the collectives at the end of the year, they paid off their debts from food and cash loans. However, as indicated above, many peasants' annual expenditure exceeded their income. The result was debts to the collectives.

The debt problem resulted from two related structural factors. First, the terms of trade between agricultural products and industrial goods did not favor agriculture. Although the price of some industrial goods decreased considerably during the collective era, the procurement price of most agricultural goods was kept relatively low to facilitate accumulation. The price of agricultural goods was not fixed or decreasing, but overall increased only moderately during the collective era. Take rice as an example: between 1965 and 1978, the procurement price in Songzi increased just 0.9 percent annually.[57] Furthermore, the productivity increase in agriculture was always slower than in industry, which put agricultural goods at a disadvantage.

Second, within their very limited income, the rural collectives had to cover various expenditures, including medical care, capital investment, and the basic needs of all the members. This further limited the available resources for consumption. Returning to the accounts of the Yongjiu brigade team, we see that in 1981 the total revenue of the team was 77,229.51 yuan. A portion of this revenue was used to cover production costs (fertilizer, seeds, machines, taxes, etc.); another portion was reserved for public welfare accumulation and a capital improvement fund. The costs totaled 31,410.61 yuan, leaving 39,915.37 yuan for distribution to members according to their work points. However, the total actually allocated was 42,689.97 yuan, because that was the total consumption needed by the peasants. This means a new debt of 2,774.6 was added to the team's accumulated debts from previous years.

The persistent indebtedness was not surprising in a poor country attempting to build its own modern industry, since it could only extract surplus from itself. Paul Baran already foresaw that at the early stage of a progressive economy, mass consumption should rise very slowly, if at all. Indeed, it was an advantage for the peasants to have collectives from which they could always borrow with no interest.[58] Moreover, in my interviews, none of the older peasants ever expressed discontent with the pro-accumulation policy, but tended to think of themselves as allied with industrial workers. That is, they believed China needed to build its industry, with the support of agriculture. Once industry got stronger, industry could support agriculture with its technology and capital, and both would be developed.

The other side of the story is the existence of income differentials within collectives, which is in immediate conflict with the official ideology. In fact, as Whyte observed, China's egalitarianism was more evident on an ideological level and less at the level of reducing income differentials.[59] However, this may not have been a serious problem. Income distribution under the collectives was definitely much more equal than in the Republican period.[60] Furthermore, household income was affected by the number of laborers and dependents, which means that high-income households might have a lot of people to feed. Thus, household income differentials did not necessarily translate into a high degree of inequality.

Intracollective inequalities also stemmed from other sources. For example, differences in per capita income among collectives may also occur as a result of differences in quantity and quality of land per head, which is largely a legacy from the revolution and land reform.[61] As production teams became the basic accounting units after the early 1960s, very limited inter-team redistribution occurred, which contributed to the differences among teams, brigades, and communes. Vermeer similarly observed that the size of the economic accounting unit also had a major influence on inequality.[62]

DECOLLECTIVIZATION

Rumors circulated at the beginning of the 1980s about possible changes in the Communist Party's rural policies. It was later confirmed that household production was the new favored model of the central leaders. In fact, some villages had already adopted household farming as early as 1980 under orders from above.[63] In 1981, Du Runsheng, the architect of decollectivization at the national level, went to a national council meeting with all the ministers in 1981 to present ideas for reforming the collectives.[64] In his critique of the rural collectives, Du emphasized that the existing collectives were not really egalitarian. On the one hand, some privileged groups appropriated an unfair share of the surplus; on the other hand, 31 percent of the households were in debt. Du's talk seemed to be well received by the top leaders, and Bo Yibo, the vice premier, immediately commented, "This is also exploitation!" It should be noted that this meeting was clearly organized to announce the upcoming decollectivization and everyone present knew it. It is interesting that the politicians actually considered stratification rather than "egalitarianism" as the core problem. But their prescription was simply to dismantle the collectives.

In late 1982, the county government sent the decollectivization order to every commune, brigade, and team. It was a very strange moment, and many peasants were simply confused.[65] A number of peasants in my interviews said the same thing. They felt the Communist Party had chosen a capitalist road by dismantling the collectives and restoring a petty producer economy. There were practical as well as ideological concerns. In those communes where mechanization was already developed and quality of life was relatively high, there was strong opposition to decollectivization. Similar hostile attitudes could also be found among families with few male laborers.[66] A peasant explained why his team was hostile to the new policy: "We already had very clear labor division: some only driving vehicles, some only cultivating, and some running the manufacturing shops, and it worked pretty well. After decollectivization, everyone had to cultivate while lots of us just did not know anything about it."[67] Another peasant shared his experiences: "By that time I was already working in another village specializing in fishery. I really loved the job, but after decollectivization my wife could not manage the plots on her own, so I had to return to my village to continue cultivating."[68]

There were certainly people who were in favor of the institutional change, including families with plenty of labor power to exploit or those in dysfunctional collectives.[69] For those who suffered from stratification, too, decollectivization seemed to be a good solution. There were even peasants who felt happy about decollectivization because they "don't have to work so hard as under collectives"![70] The illusion that decollectivization could cure the pains of stratification was so popular that it was reflected in all kinds of popular writing. In 1981, He Shiguang published an influential short story, "Xiang chang shang" [On the ground]. The gist was that, once you offended a cadre, you offended the whole elite class in the village, which would immediately create troubles for you in purchasing basic goods from the shop or in getting subsidized food (a scarce resource at that time) from the cadres. The whole village seemed to be owned and managed by a small group of people, and one had no choice but to obey their orders. So what could save the peasants? The main character explains: "I was extremely poor and ashamed, but now it is different. I am now cultivating a plot on my own, and I am now able to feed my family very well. I won't need any subsidized food from you, and you won't be able to order me around anymore." In other words, decollectivization equals political empowerment.[71]

There was also another attitude among peasants: indifference. A large portion of them did not care about ideology. What they did every day in the collectives was to get work points, and what they did after decollectivization was to earn profits. For them, socialist collectives were not bad, although not perfect; the household model would be something uncertain and might evolve into capitalism, but why bother resisting? If the policy changed, they could live with it. The only important thing for them was working hard; institutional change would be something totally exogenous. A former cadre gave this estimation of the relative portions of the different attitudes in his brigade: more than 30 percent against decollectivization, less than 30 percent in favor of decollectivization, and the remaining 40 percent were fine with either one.[72]

Maybe the "indifferent" people were the really wise ones, because no matter what the peasants thought, decollectivization was forced upon them by the upper-level cadres in Songzi in late 1982. Peasants and cadres described the campaign as a "wind" after which no collectives remained. Many local cadres had a very difficult time persuading themselves to agree with decollectivization; an old cadre recalled that one day he and other rural leaders were summoned to the county government to get some training on understanding the importance of decollectivization. After the training, everyone was required to swear that he or she understood the new policy and would implement it right away.[73]

It is fair to say that the ultimate reason for decollectivization in Songzi was the change of national policy, which aroused complicated reactions from the peasants depending on the relative development level of their collectives. But there was no major unrest in the process, unlike the response to reform of the publicly owned enterprises a decade later. This suggests that decollectivization indeed appealed to the peasants to some extent. What was the appeal? Stratification was at the root of unsatisfactory performance and was the focus of peasants' complaints during the collective era. Decollectivization seemed to be able to destroy stratification by destroying the collectives. That was probably one of the most important reasons for most peasants to accept the new policy without serious opposition. Farmers' incomes rose because the government raised the prices they received for their agricultural produce, which probably also contributed to the peasants' faith in the new policies. Other factors like propaganda efforts also played a role, as we have seen in previous chapters.

The question then arises, was decollectivization a genuine solution to stratification? As we note earlier in the book, stratification is not dependent on a collective structure per se. In fact, if the socialist elements of the collectives still put some constraint on stratification, at least in terms of income distribution, there would be no such restrictions afterward. In Xiliu Village, where Zhou Xianyin killed his wife, the collective enterprises, orange farms, and tea farms once performed well under Zhou. One peasant commented: "Zhou never took a dime out of the public funds."[74] However, these collective businesses all went bankrupt after decollectivization, with only the nouveaux riches benefiting. The villagers all felt that it was not possible to carry on the collective projects because nobody would take care of them.[75] In the late 1990s, the party secretary rented out large areas of farmland to some outside firms at amazingly low prices. When the peasants forced him to step down, he immediately found a new job in one of those firms.[76]

On a more general level, the investment and social support that the peasants derived from the collective businesses were severely eroded after decollectivization.[77] Although critical of the rural collectives, Friedman et al. admitted that the post-Mao era did not show any "signs of change for the better" and that under the collective regime "privileged people monopolized material perquisites behind closed doors," while in the post-collective era "wealth was flaunted."[78] The uprising in Wukan after more than a decade of grievances illustrates that decollectivization actually disempowered the peasantry and allowed even greater and more explicit stratification.[79]

Epilogue

The dramatic political and economic change in the Chinese villages in the 1980s was a prelude to the many struggles that finally gave birth to contemporary Chinese society. The seemingly harmonious ending of collectives and the subsequent output spur have provided political and economic conditions for the later rise of capitalism in China.

Theoretically, the success story of decollectivization in China is part of the basis of neoliberal doctrine. The neoliberal doctrine holds privatization and market liberalization as the prescription for a prosperous human society. Mainstream ideology also considers decollectivization and the neoliberal reforms in general as spontaneous grassroots movements. This line is explicitly or implicitly embedded in most of the contemporary writing on China's recent history.

This book looks critically at the Chinese agrarian change from a Marxist point of view. Based on both quantitative and qualitative evidence, I show that the decollectivization campaign did not happen because of inefficient collectives and did not lead to more efficient agriculture. The campaign was more top-down and coercive than spontaneous and grassroots-based. After debunking the myth, I argue that it was vital for the post-Mao elites to dismantle the collectives to pursue a pro-capitalist path and that decollectivization served as the very first step in cracking the Maoist system. This is not saying the Maoist collectives were perfect socialist models. The case study at the end focuses on the contradictions within the collectives, which helps explain the puzzle that a potentially unpopular reform such as decollectivization did not meet much opposition from the collective members.

The last decade has clearly seen a revival of Marxism in both academic and activist circles in China. I taught economics in colleges in China for three years after graduate school. I often included in my syllabus the political economy of decollectivization. The students loved to hear a Marxist (and different) explanation of decollectivization and the broad social change in China. My feeling is that the official propaganda about decollectivization is less popular than before. I take that as a sign of a shift in the mind-set of Chinese youth toward China's socialist past and capitalist present. In the last decade, a new generation of radical scholars has emerged in China, including Lao Tian and She Shui Nong Fu, who have published many critical essays on agrarian change on major leftist websites. A popular activist-scholar-based website, People's Food Sovereignty (www.shiwuzq.com), has also published important critiques on the capitalist transformation of agriculture.

After all, the rural working people did not gain much besides praise on paper about their "initiative" in tearing down socialism. Actually, no working people in the world have gained much. We are at a particularly interesting time when nearly forty years of neoliberalism has created its own systemic crisis and made working people's lives even harder around the whole world. The question, of course, is, what is to be done?

It is now clear that the traditional peasant question will fade and the worker question will become dominant in China. The current Chinese regime encourages land consolidation and further privatization of the rural land. This trend is complicated by efforts to maintain a safety network for the migrant workers by preserving small household production. But overall, capitalism has already begun and will

Epilogue

continue to dominate the Chinese countryside. There is no visible feudal relation emerging there, and the traditional peasant question (redistributive land reform) is no longer a major concern. On the other hand, the conflict between workers (the old urban workers, the new migrant workers, and the rural workers) and the industrial and agrarian capitalists is becoming increasingly significant.

In the current context, a progressive economic program in China will have to include at least the following. First of all, (re)empower the peasants by organizing peasants into peasant associations and co-ops. The decollectivization has left millions of peasants greatly disempowered. This could help to reduce the exploitation of middlemen and big capital and stop the deterioration of the living conditions of the millions of rural residents.

Second, rebuild the peasant-worker alliance both in terms of economics and politics. One of the lessons from the last century is that peasants and workers did not have much solidarity in their resistance to neoliberalism. The ruling class took advantage of this and let the migrant peasant workers compete with the urban workers to enforce discipline and to lower wages. A rise in peasants' income and workers' wages at the same time will make sure that they are not again divided and conquered. In this way, any blessing for the peasants (for example, higher grain prices) will not turn into a curse for the workers (higher living costs). Currently workers and peasants are still struggling with different issues, but in due time there might emerges more political collaboration between the two.

Third, capital regulation and control are crucial. The neoliberal age has given capital the freedom to move across borders to achieve a greater profit, and it has given the working class the freedom to race to the bottom. If pro-peasant-worker policies are to be implemented, tight controls on capital flow will be a necessary condition so that the capitalists cannot easily run away from their responsibilities as they often do in the neoliberal age.

There are still many unsettled questions in this book on building and maintaining a better society. Alain Badiou says we are still the contemporaries of May 1968. He is absolutely correct in the sense that the last generation has not fully solved the questions arising from the last wave of revolutionary experiments. Any future socialist project will have to revisit the history of socialism in the last century. The capitalist class has fruitlessly sought to return to the prerevolutionary phase, providing literally nothing valuable for building a better society. The working class of the world cannot afford to waste more time on capitalism. It is time to ask these questions again.

APPENDIX 1

APPENDIX 2

BIBLIOGRAPHY

Appendix 1

DETAILS OF THE REPLICATION OF LIN'S PAPER IN CHAPTER 3

The core model in Lin's paper is shown in Equation 1. It is a typical Cobb-Douglas production function with total real-crop values as output and four input variables: land, labor, power, and chemical fertilizer. In addition, six ad hoc variables were included: the proportion of teams that had adopted HRS at the end of the year (HRS), the index of market price relative to manufactured input price (MP), the index of above-quota prices relative to industrial input prices (GP, from Table 3.3, col. 3), the percentage of sown area in nongrain crops (Ngca), the multiple-crop index (MCI), and a time trend (T).[1] Twenty-eight provincial dummies were included to account for unobserved soil, cultural, and political factors. Lin also did a two-way fixed-effect model and included time dummies to capture year-specific factors such as weather and price changes.[2] Both one-way and two-way fixed-effect models are replicated in Table 3.4, columns 1 and 2.

---

1. The appendix of Lin's paper gave a detailed explanation of the sources of these data.
2. National price ratio index variables are dropped to avoid colinearity.

$$\text{Ln}(Y_{i,t}) = \alpha_1 + \alpha_2 * \text{Ln}(\text{Land}_{i,t}) + \alpha_3 * \text{Ln}(\text{Labor}_{i,t}) + \alpha_4 * \text{Ln}(\text{Power}_{i,t})$$
$$+ \alpha_5 * \text{Ln}(\text{Fert}_{i,t}) + \alpha_6 * \text{Ln}(\text{MP}_{i,t-1}) + \alpha_7 * \text{Ln}(\text{GP}_{it}) + \alpha_8 * \text{Ln}(\text{Ngca}_{it})$$
$$+ \alpha_9 * \text{Ln}(\text{MCI}_{it}) + \alpha_{10} * \text{HRS}_{i,t} + \alpha_{11} * T_t + \sum_{i=0}^{27} a_j D_j + \varepsilon_{it}$$

Where Y = crop output per team in constant 1980 prices
Land = cultivated land per team
Labor = weighted labor force per team
Power = total power used (machines and draft animals)
Fert = Fertilizer application per team

Here we estimate the effect of HRS by adjusting Lin's model based on the critiques laid out in the text. Before the empirical analysis, the adjustments need to be operationalized.

First, as this study argues, before any detailed data illustrating the actual HRS adoption rate before yearly production became available, it seems to be more appropriate to use a one-period lagged value of HRS. This way, all the production progress attributed to HRS in the model would be justified. Second, a two-way fixed-effect model seems to be the more reliable specification; therefore it will continue to be used by this study. This also implies that the problematic price index used by Lin will not become a problem here because it will be dropped and the price impacts will be captured by year dummies. Third, weather conditions (data is from Table 3.2) will be added into the model to see if the year dummies could fully capture its impacts. The basic model is shown in Equation 2 as a two-way fixed-effect model with almost the same variables as Lin used (see last section for variable explanation).

$$\text{Ln}(Y_{i,t}) = \alpha_1 + \alpha_2 * \text{Ln}(\text{Land}_{i,t}) + \alpha_3 * \text{Ln}(\text{Labor}_{i,t}) + \alpha_4 \text{Ln}(\text{Power}_{i,t}) + \alpha_5 * \text{Ln}(\text{Fert}_{i,t}) + \alpha_6 * \text{Ln}(\text{Ngca}_{i,t}) + \alpha_7 * \text{Ln}(\text{MCI}_{i,t})$$
$$+ \alpha_8 * \text{HRS}_{i,t} + \alpha_9 * T_t + \sum_{j=0}^{27} a_j D_j + \sum_{k=0}^{17} a_k T_k + \varepsilon_{i,t}$$

Appendix 1

The results are illustrated in columns 3 and 4 of Table 3.4; the first model does not take weather into consideration whereas the second does.

Are our results robust? In particular, we are interested in the effect of HRS if part of end-of-year HRS did have some impact on that year's productivity. In other words, if Lin showed the most favorable case of HRS, the above exercises just illustrate a not so favorable scenario. But in case the true scenario was between the two extremes, some sensitivity test is needed to better understand the role of HRS. Eleven alternative HRS measures are constructed as weighted averages of consecutive years' HRS values. The first HRS (hrs0) measure is the same as Lin (1992), which assigns zero weight for the previous year's HRS; the weight for the previous year's HRS increases 10 percent each time, and the last measure (hrs10) is just the same with one-year lagged HRS. The results are presented in Table A1 (see below), which singles out the coefficients and T values of HRS measure. As the weight for the previous year's HRS increases, which implies more decollectivization took place in the latter half of the year, the effect of HRS decreases steadily. From hrs5, which means process of decollectivization distributed equally between the first and second half of the year, HRS ceases to be significant statistically. Given our previous discussions on the pace of decollectivization in China, it is more plausible to assume that more than half of the production teams adopted HRS in the second half of a given year, which in turn suggests that it is more likely that HRS did not make a significant contribution to productivity changes. The sensitivity test adds more confidence to our conclusion.

TABLE A1: Sensitivity Test

	Coefficient	T Value
hrs 0*	0.15	3.00
hrs 1*	0.15	2.29
hrs 2*	0.15	2.23
hrs 3*	0.14	2.12
hrs 4*	0.13	2.03
hrs 5	0.12	1.89
hrs 6	0.11	1.75
hrs 7	0.09	1.64
hrs 8	0.08	1.47
hrs 9	0.07	1.37
hrs 10	0.06	1.22

*Significant at 5% level.

Appendix 2

LIST OF PEOPLE INTERVIEWED

Person #1	Peasant in a former state farm
Person #2	Current party secretary of a village
Person #3	Peasant and longtime cadre
Person #4	Peasant and former team accountant
Person #5	Former peasant and retired worker from a coal mine
Person #6	Longtime rural cadre
Person #7	Current party secretary of a village
Person #8	Peasant and former team head
Person #9	Peasant and former accountant
Person #10	Former peasant and tailor in a commune
Person #11	Peasant and Person #9's spouse
Person #12	Peasant in a former state farm
Person #13	Peasant in a former state farm
Person #14	Peasant and longtime cadre
Person #15	Peasant-cadre
Person #16	Peasant and Person #14's spouse
Person #17	Peasant and Person #26's spouse
Person #18	Peasant

Person #19	Former team head
Person #20	Longtime peasant-cadre
Person #21	Peasant
Person #22	Famous national model of peasants in Mao's time; longtime cadre
Person #23	Former teacher in a brigade school
Person #24	Local cadre, born in a peasant family
Person #25	Longtime rural cadre
Person #26	Peasant
Person #27	Longtime peasant-cadre
Person #28	Longtime peasant-cadre
Person #29	Cadre in party municipal office of Songzi
Person #30	Longtime peasant and Person #27's spouse
Person #31	Current party vice secretary of a village
Person #32	Longtime rural cadre
Person #33	Longtime peasant-cadre
Person #34	Former blacksmith in a commune's factory

Bibliography

Akram-Lodhi, A. Haroon. "Land Markets and Rural Livelihoods in Vietnam." In *Land, Poverty and Livelihoods in an Era of Globalization: Perspectives from Developing and Transition Countries*, edited by H. Akram-Lodhi, S. J. Borras, and C. Kay, 152–187. London and New York: Routledge, 2007.

——— and Cristóbal Kay. "Surveying the Agrarian Question (Part 1): Unearthing Foundations, Exploring Diversity." *Journal of Peasant Studies* 37 (2010): 177–202.

Andreas, J. *Rise of the Red Engineers: The Cultural Revolution and the Origins of China's New Class*. Redwood City, CA: Stanford University Press, 2009.

Aubert, Claude. "The Agricultural Crisis in China at the End of the 1980s." In *Remaking Peasant China: Problems of Rural Development and Institutions at the Start of the 1990s*, edited by J. Delman, C. S. Ostergaard, and F. Christiansen, 16–37. Denmark: Aarhus University Press, 1990.

Bai, Shi. "Wo cong fuchuji yibu kuajin shengwei changwei" [Huge promotion to provincial standing committee]. *Yanhuang Chunqiu* 7 (2007): 6–11.

Baran, P. A. *The Political Economy of Growth*. New York: Monthly Review Press, 1962.

Barraclough, Solon L. "Land Reform in Developing Countries: The Role of the State and Other Actors." Geneva: UNRISD, 1999.

Beijing Difangzhi Committee. *Beijingzhi: nongyejuan nongcun jingji zonghezhi* [Beijing rural economy records]. Beijing: Beijing Chubanshe, 2008.
Bernstein, Henry. "Agrarian Questions Then and Now." *Journal of Peasant Studies* 24 (1996): 22–59.
Bernstein, Henry. "Land Reform: Taking a Long(er) View." *Journal of Agrarian Change* 2 (2002): 433–463.
Bernstein, Henry. " 'Changing Before Our Very Eyes': Agrarian Questions and the Politics of Land in Capitalism Today." *Journal of Agrarian Change* 4 (2004): 190–225.
Bernstein, Thomas. "Farmer Discontent and Regime Responses." In *The Paradox of China's Post-Mao Reforms,* edited by M. Goldman and R. MacFarquhar, 197–219. Cambridge, MA: Harvard University Press, 1999.
Bi, Y., and Z. Zheng. "The Actual Changes of Cultivated Area since the Founding of New China." *Resource Science* 22, no. 2 (2000): 8–12.
Blecher, Marc. "Income Distribution in Small Rural Chinese Communities." *China Quarterly* 68 (1976): 797–816.
Bo, Yibo. *Ruogan zhongda juece yu shijian de huigu* [Reflections on several significant events and decisions]. Beijing: Renmin Chubanshe, 1997.
Borras, S. Jr., Cristóbal Kay, and A. Haroon Akram-Lodhi. "Agrarian Reform and Rural Development: Historical Overview and Current Issues." In *Land, Poverty and Livelihoods in an Era of Globalization,* 1–40.
Boukaraoun, Hacene. "The Privatization Process in Algeria." *Developing Economies* 29 (1991): 89–124.
Bramall, Chris. "Origins of the Agricultural 'Miracle': Some Evidence from Sichuan." *China Quarterly* 143 (1995): 731–755.
Bramall, Chris. *Sources of Chinese Economic Growth, 1978–1996.* New York: Oxford University Press, 2000.
Brass, Tom. "Latin American Peasants: New Paradigms for Old?" *Journal of Peasant Studies* 29 (2002): 1–40.
Bush, Ray. "Mubarak's Legacy for Egypt's Rural Poor: Returning Land to the Landlords." In *Land, Poverty and Livelihoods in an Era of Globalization,* 254–283.
Carolus, Carol. "Sources of Chinese Agricultural Growth in the 1980s." PhD diss., Boston University, 1992.
Chan, A., R. Madsen, and J. Unger. *Chen Village Under Mao and Deng.* Oakland: University of California Press, 1992.

Commission of the Central Committee of the CPSU(B). *History of Communist Party of Soviet Union (Bolsheviks)*. New York: International Publishers, 1939.

Daley, Elizabeth. "Land and Social Change in a Tanzanian Village 1: Kinyanambo, 1920s–1990." *Journal of Agrarian Change* 5 (2005): 363–404.

Das, R. J. "The Spatiality of Class and State Power: The Case of India's Land Reforms." *Environment and Planning* A31 (1999): 2103–2126.

———. "Looking, but Not Seeing: The State and/as Class in Rural India." *Journal of Peasant Studies* 34 (2007): 408–440.

de Janvry, Alain, Elisabeth Sadoulet, and Wendy Wolford. 1998. "From State-Led to Grassroots-Led Land Reform in Latin America." In *Access to Land, Rural Poverty and Public Action*, edited by Alain de Janvry, Gustavo Gordillo, Jean-Philippe Platteau, and Elisabeth Sadoulet, 279–315. Oxford: Oxford University Press, 2001.

Deng, Xiaoping. *Selected Works of Deng Xiaoping (1975–1982)*. Beijing: Foreign Languages Press, 1984.

——— *Deng Xiaoping wenxuan* [Selected works of Deng Xiaoping], vol. 2. Beijing: Renmin Chubanshe, 1994.

———. "Zenyang huifu nongye shengchan" [How to restore agricultural production]. In *Deng Xiaoping wenxuan* [Selected works of Deng Xiaoping], vol. 1. Beijing: Renmin Chubanshe, 1962/1994.

Deng, Zihui. *Deng Zihui wenji* [Collected works of Deng Zihui]. Beijing: Renmin Chubanshe, 2006.

Dikötter, F. *Mao's Great Famine: The History of China's Most Devastating Catastrophe, 1958–1962*. New York: Walker & Company, 2010.

Du, Runsheng. "Nongcun shengchan zerenzhi yu nongcun jingji tizhi gaige" [Rural responsibility system and rural economic reform]. *Hongqi* 19(1981): 383.

———. *Dangdai zhongguo de nongye hezuozhi* [Collective agriculture in modern China]. Beijing: Dangdai Zhongguo Chubanshe, 2002.

———. *Du Rusheng zishu* [Du Runsheng's recollections]. Beijing: Renmin Chubanshe, 2005.

El-Ghonemy, M. R. "The Political Economy of Market Based Land Reform." Geneva: UNRISD, 1999.

———. *The Crisis of Rural Poverty and Hunger: An Essay on the Complementarity between Market- and Government-Led Land Reform for Its Resolution*. New York: Routledge, 2007.

Fan, Shenggen, and Xiaobo Zhang. "Production and Productivity Growth in Chinese Agriculture: New National and Regional

Measures." *Economic Development and Cultural Change* 50, no. 4 (2002): 819–838.

Foster, J. B., R.W. McChesney, and R. J. Jonna. "The Global Reserve Army of Labor and the New Imperialism." *Monthly Review* 63 (2011): 1–31.

Friedman, E., P. G. Pickowicz, and M. Selden. *Revolution, Resistance, and Reform in Village China*. New Haven, CT: Yale University Press, 2007.

Fujian Difangzhi Committee. *Fujianshengzhi gongchandangzhi* [Fujian communist party records]. Beijing: Zhongguo Shehui Kexue Chubanshe, 1999.

Griffin, Keith, and Ashwani Saith. "The Pattern of Income Inequality in Rural China." *Oxford Economic Papers* 34, no. 1 (1982): 172–206.

Han, Dongping. *The Unknown Cultural Revolution: Life and Change in a Chinese Village*. New York: Monthly Review Press, 2008.

Hartford, Kathleen. "Socialist Agriculture Is Dead: Long Live Socialist Agriculture! Organizational Transformation in Rural China." In *The Political Economy of Reform in Post-Mao China: Causes, Content, and Consequences*, edited by E. Perry and C. Wong. Cambridge, MA: Harvard University Press, 1985.

He, Shiguang. "Xiang chang shang" [On the ground]. In *1980 Nian quanguo youxiu duanpian xiaoshuo pingxuan huojiang zuopin ji* [1980 Selection of the awarded short novels], edited by Renmin Wenxue. Shanghai: Shanghai Wenyi Chubanshe, 1981.

He, Xuefeng. "Renmin gongshe de sanda gongneng" [Three functions of the People's Commune]. http: //www.snzg.cn/article/2007/1114/article_7916.html, accessed on Dec 29, 2011.

Hinnebusch, Raymond A. "The Political Economy of Economic Liberalization in Syria." *International Journal of Middle East Studies* 27 (1995): 305–320.

Han, Dongping. *The Unknown Cultural Revolution: Life and Change in a Chinese Village*. New York: Monthly Review Press, 2008.

Hinton, William. *Fanshen: A Documentary of Revolution in a Chinese Village*. London: Vintage Books, 1966.

———. *Shenfan*. New York: Random House, 1983.

———. *The Great Reversal*. New York: Monthly Review Press, 1990.

Hongqi. *Bashi niandai chu di wo guo nongye shengchan ze ren zhi: Diaocha baogao xuanbian* [Selected reports on agriculture responsibility system]. Beijing: Hongqi Chubanshe, 1984.

Hsu, D. Y., and P. Y. Ching. "The Worker-Peasant Alliance as a Strategy for Rural Development in China." *Monthly Review* 42, no. 10 (1991): 27–43.

Huang, Daoxia, Zhan Yu, and Xiyu Wang. *Jianguo yilai nongye hezuohua shiliao huibian* [Document collections on agricultural collectivization]. Beijing: Zhonggong Dangshi Chubanshe, 1992.

Huang, Philip C. *The Peasant Family and Rural Development in the Yangzi Delta, 1350–1988*. Stanford, CA: Stanford University Press, 1990.

Huang, Shu-min. *The Spiral Road: Change in a Chinese Village Through the Eyes of a Communist Party Leader*. Boulder, CO: Westview Press, 1989.

Hunan Difangzhi Committee. *Hunanshengzhi nonglinshuilizhi* [Hunan agriculture records]. Changsha: Hunan Chubanshe, 1991.

Jiang, Zilong. "Qiao changzhang shangren ji" [Qiao became the new director], *1979 Nian quanguo youxiu duanpian xiaoshuo pingxuan huojiang zuopin ji* [1979 Selection of the awarded short novels], edited by Renmin Wenxue. Shanghai: Shanghai Wenyi Chubanshe, 1979.

———. "Zihao yu beiqing: yige laogongren de shushuo" [Pride and sorrow: a recollection of an old worker]. *Tong Zhou Gong Jin*, 8 (2010).

Jilin Difangzhi Committee. *Jilinshengzhi: Nongyezhi*. Jinlin: Jinlin Renmin Chubanshe, 1993.

Jin, S., Huang, J., Hu, R., and Rozelle, S. "The Creation and Spread of Technology and Total Factor Productivity in China's Agriculture." *American Journal of Agricultural Economics* 84, no. 4 (2002): 916–930.

Kalirajan, K. P., M. B. Obwona, and S. Zhao. "A Decomposition of Total Factor Productivity Growth: The Case of Chinese Agricultural Growth Before and After Reforms." *American Journal of Agricultural Economics* 78, no. 2 (1996): 331–338.

Kay, Cristóbal. "Latin America's Agrarian Reform: Lights and Shadows." *Land Reform, Land Settlement and Cooperatives Bulletin* 1998: 8–31.

Kelliher, Daniel. *Peasant Power in China*. New Haven, CT: Yale University Press, 1992.

Kotz, David, and Fred Weir. *Russia's Path from Gorbachev to Putin: The Demise of the Soviet System and the New Russia*. New York: Routledge, 2007.

Kueh, Y. Y. *Agricultural Instability in China 1931–1991*. New York: Oxford University Press, 1995.

Kung, James Kaising. "Egalitarianism, Subsistence Provision, and Work

Incentives in China's Agricultural Collectives." *World Development* 22, no. 2 (1994): 175–187.

Lenin, V. I. *Collected Works*, vol. 25. Moscow: Progress Publishers, 1964.

Li, Changping. "Be Cautious When Talking About Land Privatization." *China Left Review* 1 (2008).

Li, Huaiyin. "Everyday Strategies for Team Farming in Collective-era China: Evidence from Qin Village." *China Journal* 54 (2005): 79–98.

———. *Village China under Socialism and Reform: A Micro History, 1948–2008*. Stanford, CA: Stanford University Press, 2009.

Lin, Justin Yifu. "The Household Responsibility System in China's Agricultural Reform: A Theoretical and Empirical Study." *Economic Development and Cultural Change* 36, no. 3 (1988): S199–S224.

———. "Rural Reforms and Agricultural Growth in China." *American Economic Review* 82, no. 1 (1992): 34–51.

Liu, Suinian, and Qungan Wu. *Wenhuadageming shiqi de guominjingji* [Economy in the Cultural Revolution]. Harbin: Heilongjiang Renmin Chubanshe, 1986.

Ma, Liqun, and Zhijun Lin. *Jiaofeng* (Crossing Swords). Beijing: Beijing Jin Ri Zhongguo Chubanshe:,1998.

Ma, Shexiang. *Qianzou: 1965 Mao Zedong chongshang jinggang shan* [Prelude: Mao's 1965 revisit to Jinggang Mountain]. Dangdai Zhongguo Chubanshe, 2006.

MacFarquhar, R. *Origins of the Cultural Revolution*, vol. 1. New York: Oxford University Press, 1974.

———. *Origins of the Cultural Revolution*, vol. 3. New York: Columbia University Press, 1997.

———, ed. "The Succession to Mao and the End of Maoism, 1969–82." *The Politics of China: The Eras of Mao and Deng*, 248–339. Cambridge, UK: Cambridge University Press. 1997.

——— and M. Schoenhals. *Mao's Last Revolution*. Cambridge: Belknap Press, 2006.

McMillan, John, John Whalley, and Lijing Zhu. "The Impact of China's Economic Reforms on Agricultural Productivity Growth." *Journal of Political Economy* 97, no. 4 (1989): 781–807.

Magdoff, Harry. "China: Contrasts with the USSR." *Monthly Review* 27 (1975): 12–57.

Mao, Zedong. "Report on an Investigation of the Peasant Movement in Hunan." *Selected Works of Mao Tse-tung*, vol. 1, 23–59. Beijing: Foreign Languages Press, 1926/1965.

———. "On the Co-operative Transformation of Agriculture." *Selected*

Works of Mao Tse-tung, vol. 5, 184–207. Beijing: Foreign Languages Press, 1955/1977.

———. *Maozedong du shehuizhuyi zhengzhijingjixue pizhu he tanhua* [Mao on socialist political economy]. Beijing: Zhonghua renmin gongheguo guoshi xuehui, 1998.

Mathijs, Erik, and Johan F. M. Swinnen. "The Economics of Agricultural Decollectivization in East Central Europe and the Former Soviet Union." *Economic Development and Cultural Change* 47 (1998): 1–26.

Meisner, Maurice. *Mao's China and After: A History of the People's Republic*. New York: Simon and Schuster, 1999.

Metz, Helen Chapin. "Iraq: A Country Study." Washington, DC: Library of Congress, 1988. https://www.loc.gov/resource/frdcstdy.iraqcountrystudy00metz_0.

Ministry of Agriculture. *Xin zhongguo nongye 60nian tongji ziliao* [Agricultural statistics of China's 60 years]. Beijing: Zhongguo Nongye Chubanshe, 2009.

Ostergaard, Clemens Stubbe. "Introduction." In *Remaking Peasant China: Problems of Rural Development and Institutions at the Start of the 1990s,* edited by J. Delman, C. S. Ostergaard, and F. Christiansen. Aarhus, Denmark: Aarhus University Press, 1990.

Pang, Xianzhi, and Chongji Jin. "Mao Zedong zhuan: 1949–1976" [A biography of Mao Zedong]. Beijing: Zhongyang Wenxian Chubanshe, 2003.

Patnaik, Utsa. "On Famine and Measuring 'Famine Deaths.'" In *Thinking Social Science in India: Essays in Honour of Alice Thorner*, edited by J. B. Sujata Patel, 46–68. Mumbai: Krishna Raj, 2002.

Peng, Xizhe. "Demographic Consequences of the Great Leap Forward in China's Provinces." *Population and Development Review* 13, no. 4 (1987): 639–670.

Petras, James, and Henry Veltmeyer. "Are Latin American Peasant Movements Still a Force for Change? Some New Paradigms Revisited." *Journal of Peasant Studies* 28 (2001): 83–118.

Potter, Sulamith, and Jack Potter. *China's Peasants: The Anthropology of a Revolution*. New York: Cambridge University Press, 1990.

Putterman, Louis. *Continuity and Change in China's Rural Development*. New York: Oxford University Press, 1993.

———. "Ration Subsidies and Incentives in the Pre-Reform Chinese Commune." *Economica* 55, no. 218 (1988): 235–247.

———. "Entering the Post-Collective Era in North China: Dahe Township." *Modern China* 15, no. 3 (1989): 275–320.

Riskin, Carl. "Maoism and Motivation: Work Incentives in China." In *China's Uninterrupted Revolution*, edited by V. Nee and J. Peck, 415–461. New York: Pantheon Books, 1975
———. *China's Political Economy: The Quest for Development since 1949*. New York: Oxford University Press, 1987.
———. "Seven Questions About the Chinese Famine of 1959–1961." *China Economic Review* 9, no. 2 (1998): 111–124.
Saith, Ashwani. "From Collectives to Markets: Restructured Agriculture-Industry Linkages in Rural China: Some Micro-level Evidence." *Journal of Peasant Studies* 22, no. 2 (1995): 201–260.
———. "China and India: The Institutional Roots of Differential Performance." *Development and Change* 39, no. 5 (2008): 723–757.
Sen, Amartya. "Remarks at the Inaugural Meeting of the GDN Conference on Understanding Reform." New Delhi: Global Development Conference, January 27, 2004.
Shanghai Nongyezhi Committee. *Shanghai nongyezhi* [Shanghai agriculture records]. Shanghai: Shanghai Shehui Kexueyuan Chubanshe, 1996.
Sicular, T. (1988). "Agricultural Planning and Pricing in the Post-Mao Period." *China Quarterly*, (No. 116): 671–705.
Songzi Shizhi Committee. *Songzi shizhi* [Local Records of Songzi, 1986–2005]. Songzi: Songzi Shizhi Committee, 2011.
Songzi Water Bureau. *Songzi shuilizhi* [History of water utilization]. Beijing: Zhongguo Huanjing Kexue Chubanshe, 2008.
Songzi Xianzhi Committee. *Songzi xianzhi* [Local records of Songzi, 1949–1985]. Songzi: Songzi Xianzhi Committee, 1986.
State Development and Reform Committee. "1953–2003 Sanzhong liangshi pingjun chengbenshouyi huibian" [Cost and revenue statistics of three main grain crops 1953–2003]. http://www.npcs.gov.cn.
State Statistical Bureau (SSB). *Xinzhongguo 55 nian tongji ziliao huibian* [China Compendium of Statistics, 1949–2004]. Beijing: Zhongguo Tongji Chubanshe, 2005.
———. *Xinzhongguo 60 nian tongji ziliao huibian* [China Compendium of Statistics, 1949–2008]. Beijing: Zhongguo Tongji Chubanshe, 2010.
———. *China Statistical Yearbook*. Beijing: Zhongguo Tongji Chubanshe, 2012.
Stone, B. "Developments in Agricultural Technology." *China Quarterly*, no. 116 (1988): 767–822.
Tan, Tongxue. "Zhuanxing xiangcun de daode, quanli yu shehui jiegou (Morality, Power, and Social Structure in the Transition of

Rural Society)." PhD diss., Huazhong University of Science and Technology, 2007.
Tao, Lujia. *Mao zhuxi jiao women dang shengwei shuji* [Chairman Mao teaches us how to work as provincial party secretary]. Beijing: Zhongyang Wenxian Chubanshe, 1996.
Tawney, Richard Henry. *Land and Labor in China*. Armonk, NY: M. E. Sharpe, 1966.
Teiwes, Frederick. "The Establishment and Consolidation of the New Regime, 1949–1957." In *The Politics of China: The Eras of Mao and Deng*, edited by R. MacFarquhar, 5–86. Cambridge, UK: Cambridge University Press, 1997.
Thorner, Alice. "Semi-Feudalism or Capitalism? Contemporary Debate on Classes and Modes of Production in India." *Economic and Political Weekly* 17 (1982): 49–51.
Tian, Yonghua. *Chun feng man juan* [Spring winds come]. Wuhan: Changjiang Wenyi Chubanshe, 2008.
Unger, Jonathan. "The Decollectivization of the Chinese Countryside: A Survey of Twenty-eight Villages." *Pacific Affairs* 58, no. 4 (1985): 585–606.
U.S. Department of Agriculture. "Agricultural Statistics of the People's Republic of China, 1949–90." The Róbinson Rojas Archive, 1992. http://www.rrojasdatabank.info/90010.htm, accessed February 20, 2014.
Vermeer, E. B. "Income Differentials in Rural China." *China Quarterly* 89 (1982): 1–33.
wa Githinji, Mwangi, and Gebru Mersha. "Untying the Gordian Knot: The Question of Land Reform in Ethiopia." In *Land, Poverty and Livelihoods in an Era of Globalization*, 310–343.
Wang, Guichen, and Qiren Zhou. *Smashing the Communal Pot*. Beijing: New World Press, 1985.
Wang, Shaoguang. "Failure of Charisma: The Cultural Revolution in Wuhan." PhD diss., Cornell University, 1990.
Wang, Yanhai. "Kuachu diyibu hao Jianxin" [Hard to make the first step]. *Jianghuai Wenshi* 4 (2007): 117–129.
Wang, Zhenqi. "Huyaobang yanli piping 'dingmengang' " [Hu Yaobang harshly criticizes "blocks"]. *Shi Ji Qiao* 12 (2011): 45–47.
Wen, Dale. "How to Feed China: A Tale of Two Paradigms." *Third World Resurgence* (April 2008): 212.
Wen, Guanzhong James. "Total Factor Productivity Change in China's Farming Sector: 1952–1989." *Economic Development and Cultural Change* 42, no. 1 (1993): 1–41.

Wen, Tiejun. *Jiegou xiandaihua* [Deconstruct modernization]. Guangzhou: Guangdong Renmin Chubanshe, 2004.

Whyte, Martin King. "Inequality and Stratification in China." *China Quarterly* 64 (1975): 684–711.

Wu, Jinglian. "20 Nian lai gaige lilun de fazhan" [20 years' development of the theory of reform], In *20 Nian jingji gaige huigu yu zhanwang* [20 Years of economic reform: retrospect and prospect], edited by Z. Zhang, F. Huang, and G. Li. Beijing: Zhongguo Jihua Chubanshe, 1998.

Wu, Rong. "Wei zhongyang nongyanshi dagong" [Working for the central agriculture research bureau]. *Zhongshan fengyu* no. 3 (2008): 20–22.

Xu, Zhun. "The Development of Capitalist Agriculture in China." *Review of Radical Political Economics* 49, no. 4 (2017): 591–598.

———. "Decollectivization, Collective Legacy and Uneven Agricultural Development in China." *World Development* 98 (2017): 290–299.

Yan, Hairong. "The Myth of Private Ownership." *China Left Review* 1 (2008).

Yang, D. L. *Calamity and Reform in China: State, Rural Society, and Institutional Change Since the Great Leap Famine*. Stanford, CA: Stanford University Press, 1998.

Yang, Lian. "Dark Side of the Chinese Moon." *New Left Review* 32 (2005): 132–140.

Yang, Zhengwen. "Di si ci diaocha" [The fourth investigation]. *Liao Wang Zhou Kan* 8 (1984): 26–27.

Yunnan Difangzhi Committee. *Yunnan Shengzhi nongyezhi* [Yunnan Agriculture Records]. Yunnan: Yunnan Renmin Chubanshe, 1998.

Zhang, Q. Forrest, and John A. Donaldson. "From Peasants to Farmers: Peasant Differentiation, Labor Regimes, and Land-Rights Institutions in China's Agrarian Transition." *Politics & Society* 38 (2010): 458–489.

Zhao, Ziyang. *Gaige licheng* [The secret journal of Zhao Ziyang]. Hong Kong: Xinshiji Chubanshe, 2009.

Zhejiang Nongyezhi Committee. *Zhejiangsheng nongyezhi* (Zhejiang agriculture records). Zhejiang: Zhonghua Shuju, 2004.

Zhong, Funing. *The Political Economy of the Chinese Grain Marketing System*. Canberra: Australian National University, 2004. https://openresearch-repository.anu.edu.au/bitstream/1885/40548 /3/ carp_wp14.pdf.

Zhou, Caiqin. "Shan yue bu zhi xin li shi" [The innocent country moon].

1981 Nian quanguo youxiu duanpian xiaoshuo pingxuan huojiang zuopin ji [1981 Selection of the awarded short novels], edited by Renmin Wenxue. Shanghai: Shanghai Wenyi Chubanshe, 1981.

Zhou, Kate Xiao. *How the Farmers Changed China: Power of the People.* Boulder, CO: Westview Press, 1996.

Zweig, David. 1983. "Opposition to Change in Rural China: The System of Responsibility and People's Communes." *Asian Survey* 23 (1983): 879–900.

Notes

Chapter 1: Socialism and Capitalism in the Chinese Countryside

1. Zhun Xu, "The Development of Capitalist Agriculture in China," *Review of Radical Political Economics* 49, no. 4 (2017): 591-598.
2. R. MacFarquhar, *Origins of the Cultural Revolution*, vol. 1 (New York: Oxford University Press, 1974); R. MacFarquhar, "The Succession to Mao and the End of Maoism, 1969-82," in *The Politics of China: The Eras of Mao and Deng*, ed. R. MacFarquhar (Cambridge, UK: Cambridge University Press, 1997), 248-339; F. Teiwes, "The Establishment and Consolidation of the New Regime, 1949-1957," in *The Politics of China,* 5–86.
3. See, for example, Justin Yifu Lin, "Rural Reforms and Agricultural Growth in China," *American Economic Review* 82, no. 1(1992): 34–51.
4. D. L. Yang, *Calamity and Reform in China: State, Rural Society, and Institutional Change since the Great Leap Famine* (Stanford, CA: Stanford University Press, 1998).
5. For example, see D. Kelliher, *Peasant Power in China* (New Haven, CT: Yale University Press, 1992).
6. Based on Ministry of Agriculture. *Xin zhongguonongye 60nian tongjiziliao* [Agricultural statistics of China's 60 years] (Beijing: ZhongguoNongyeChubanshe, 2009).
7. Based on State Statistical Bureau, *Xinzhongguo 60 niantongjiziliaohuibian* [China Compendium of Statistics 1949–2008] (Beijing: ZhongguoNongyeChubanshe, 2010).
8. Ibid.
9. In recent research, I constructed a collective legacy index of infrastructure, education, and health care to evaluate the long-term impacts of collective agriculture on agricultural development. The empirical results suggest that the provinces with a higher collective legacy tend to have higher

agricultural productivity growth rates even after decollectivization. See Zhun Xu, "Decollectivization, Collective Legacy and Uneven Agricultural Development in China," *World Development* 98 (2017): 290–99.
10. C. Bramall, *Sources of Chinese Economic Growth, 1978–1996* (New York: Oxford University Press, 2000), 330.

Chapter 2: Chinese Agrarian Change in World-Historical Context
1. H. Bernstein, "'Changing Before Our Very Eyes': Agrarian Questions and the Politics of Land in Capitalism Today," *Journal of Agrarian Change* 4 (2004): 190–225.
2. T. Brass, "Latin American Peasants: New Paradigms For Old?" *Journal of Peasant Studies* 29 (2002): 1–40.
3. R. J. Das, "The Spatiality of Class and State Power: The Case of India's Land Reforms," *Environment and Planning* A31 (1999): 2103–2126.
4. A. Thorner, "Semi-Feudalism or Capitalism? Contemporary Debate on Classes and Modes of Production in India," *Economic and Political Weekly* 17 (1982): 49–51.
5. C. Kay, "Latin America's Agrarian Reform: Lights and Shadows," *Land Reform, Land Settlement and Cooperatives Bulletin* (1998): 8–31.
6. Ibid.
7. E. Daley, "Land and Social Change in a Tanzanian Village 1: Kinyanambo, 1920s–1990," *Journal of Agrarian Change* 5 (2005): 363–404.
8. For the case of the Soviet Union, see D. Kotz and F. Weir, *Russia's Path from Gorbachev to Putin: The Demise of the Soviet System and the New Russia* (New York: Routledge, 2007).
9. Kay, "Latin America's Agrarian Reform."
10. H. Magdoff, "China: Contrasts with the USSR," *Monthly Review* 27 (1975): 12–57.
11. M. R. El-Ghonemy, "The Political Economy of Market Based Land Reform" (Geneva: UNRISD, 1999).
12. H. Bernstein, "Land Reform: Taking a Long(er) View." *Journal of Agrarian Change* 2 (2002): 433–463.
13. See Philip C. C. Huang, Gao Yuan, and Yusheng Peng, "Capitalization Without Proletarianization in China's Agricultural Development," *Modern China* 38, no. 2 (2012): 139173; Q. Forrest Zhang and John A. Donaldson, "From Peasants to Farmers: Peasant Differentiation, Labor Regimes, and Land-Rights Institutions in China's Agrarian Transition," *Politics & Society* 38 (2010): 458–489; Zhun Xu, "The Development of Capitalist Agriculture in China."
14. M. R. El-Ghonemy, *The Crisis of Rural Poverty and Hunger: An Essay on the Complementarity Between Market- and Government-Led Land Reform for Its Resolution*, (New York: Routledge, 2007), 81; R. H. Tawney, *Land and Labor in China* (New York: M. E. Sharpe, 1966), 66.
15. Y. Bo, *Ruoganzhongdajueceyushijian de huigu* [Reflections on several significant events and decisions] (Beijing: RenminChubanshe, 1997), 198.

16. D. Huang, Zhan Yu, and Xiyu Wang, eds., *Jianguoyilainongyehezuohuashiliaohuibian* [Document collections on agricultural collectivization] (Beijing: Zhonggong Dangshi Chubanshe, 1992), 42–44.
17. See the detailed notes in Lujia Tao, *Mao zhuxijiao women dang shengweishuji* [Chairman Mao teaches us how to work as provincial party secretary] (Beijing: Zhongyang Wenxian Chubanshe, 1996), 14.
18. The term "populist" in China means the same thing in the Western context. On rural issues, it could refer to someone who favors small ownership and considers the peasantry an above-class homogenous social group. In recent years, the term has started to imply more. Since "populist" is often portrayed as defending something dying (fighting a losing battle), nowadays socialism is often categorized as populism in the mainstream media. In fact, in a recent published report on the CCP's website, one of the questions measuring populism was "Do you think that Maoist society was more egalitarian than the contemporary one?" Unsurprisingly, 40 percent of respondents answered yes. See http://theory.people.com.cn/n/2012/1206/c49152-19807772- 1.html.
19. Zihui Deng, *Deng Zihuiwenji*[Collected works of Deng Zihui] (Beijing: Renmin Chubanshe, 2006), 406–408.
20. Huang et al., "Report from the CCP South China Bureau," in *Jianguoyilainongyehezuohuashiliaohuibian*, 231–233.
21. Runsheng Du, ed., *Dangdaizhongguo de nongyehezuozhi* [Collective agriculture in modern China] (Beijing: Dangdai Zhongguo Chubanshe, 2002), 297.
22. Mao's report was delivered to provincial and county-level leaders on July 31, 1955.
23. One should not be confused by Liu's comments about "socialism after mechanization" as a socialist vision. A good example of this kind of political rhetoric is the current CCP theory about socialism as something that comes after advanced forces of production; in reality, the only function of this rhetoric is to defend the ongoing capitalist development.
24. R. MacFarquhar, *Origins of the Cultural Revolution*, vol. 3 (New York: Columbia University Press, 1997), 266.
25. Yibo Bo, *Ruoganzhongdajueceyushijian de huigu* [Reflections on several significant events and decisions] (Beijing: Renmin Chubanshe, 1997), 1078.
26. Ibid., 1074–1075.
27. Xianzhi Pang and Chongji Jin, eds., *Mao Zedong zhuan:1949–1976* [A biography of Mao Zedong] (Beijing: Zhongyang Wenxian Chubanshe, 2003), 1231.
28. This is an idiom from Sichuan Province, Deng's hometown. It is sometimes paraphrased as "white or black cat" in the media. See Deng Xiaoping, "Zenyanghuifunongyeshengchan" [How to restore agricultural production], in *Deng Xiaoping wenxuan*.
29. This term stands for small private plot, free-market exchange, small profit-oriented firms, and grain quotas contracted to individual households.

30. Shexiang Ma, *Qianzou: 1965 Mao Zedong chongshangjinggangshan* [Prelude: Mao's 1965 revisit to Jinggang Mountain) (Beijing: Dangdai Zhongguo Chubanshe, 2006), 151

31. See discussions in Athar Hussain, "Science and Technology in the Chinese Countryside," in *Science and Technology in Post-Mao China*, eds. Denis Fred Simon and Merle Goldman (Cambridge, MA: Harvard University Press, 1989); B. Stone, "Developments in Agricultural Technology," *China Quarterly* 116 (1988): 767–822; Zhun Xu, "Decollectivization, Collective Legacy, and Uneven Agricultural Development in China."

32. See Amartya Sen, "Remarks at the Inaugural Meeting of the GDN Conference on Understanding Reform," Global Development Conference, January 27 2004. There are a few studies on the social welfare programs during the collective era that illustrate how they provided basic needs with small budgets. See, for example, Dongping Han, *The Unknown Cultural Revolution: Life and Change in a Chinese Village* (New York: Monthly Review Press, 2008).

33. A. Chan, R. Madsen, and J. Unger, *Chen Village Under Mao and Deng* (Berkeley: University of California Press, 1992), 7.

34. V. I. Lenin, *Collected Works*, vol. 25 (Moscow: Progress Publishers, 1964), 471.

35. This is from Mao's talk to Premier Zhou Enlai in 1974, translated from the CCP records, http://cpc.people.com.cn/GB/64162/64164/4416102.html, accessed on 2012/09/08.

36. See the discussions about the Soviet Union in David Kotz and Fred Weir, *Russia's Path from Gorbachev to Putin: The Demise of the Soviet System and the New Russia* (New York: Routledge, 2007.

37. See Shaoguang Wang, "Failure of Charisma: The Cultural Revolution in Wuhan" (PhD diss., Cornell University, 1990), 670–684. Why the Cultural Revolution failed is another question and beyond the scope of this work.

38. There have been lots of narratives around this coup. For example, see R. MacFarquar and M. Schoenhals, *Mao's Last Revolution* (Cambridge: Belknap Press, 2006), 443–449.

39. This term was invented to refer to anything that was anti-revolutionary. For example, the *People's Daily* changed its tone to attack the movie in 1979. See Fengsong Xie, "Yingpian 'Juelie' shishenmehuose?," *People's Daily*, January 10, 1979.

40. It means "it is not our time anymore."

41. This became the most politically correct slogan in contemporary China. The new central leadership just confirmed this in the 18th National Congress of the CCP a few months ago. The "old road" could refer to the Cultural Revolution, but more generally it means both the Soviet model and the Maoist model.

42. Du came from the old populist camp and worked under Deng Zihui in the 1950s.

43. Du Runsheng, "Lianchanchengbaozhi he nongcunjingji de xinfazhan" [Household responsibility system and new development of the rural economy], *People's Daily*, March 7, 1983.
44. Du Runsheng, *Du Rushengzishu* [Du Runsheng's recollections] (Beijing: Renmin Chubanshe, 2005), 11.
45. Du Runsheng, "Zengjiatouru, fayushichang, shenhuanongcungaige." In *Sikaoyuxuanze*, ed. Du Runsheng (Beijing: Zhonggong Zhongyang-Dangxiao Chubanshe, 1990).
46. The urban-rural income ratio (defined as the urban per capita disposable income divided by the counterpart in rural areas) increased from 2.2 in 1984 to 3.1 in 2011. The share of fiscal expenditure on rural areas dropped from 13.68 percent in the 1970s to 11.80 percent in the 1980s; the medical and education system was dismantled together with the collectives. The numbers are calculated based on data from the Ministry of Agriculture (2009), and the State Statistical Bureau (2005).
47. Wen claims that the heavy population burden determines the necessity of small peasant economy. For more see Wen Tiejun, *Jiegouxiandaihua* [Deconstruct modernization] (Guangzhou: Guangdong Renmin Chubanshe, 2004), 8–22.
48. The populists would rather maintain the collective legal framework because the collective ownership makes it more difficult to buy and sell lands. So on this particular issue, many socialists and populists stand together.
49. These policies include the abolition of all agricultural taxes in 2006 and the development of a new rural medical care system after 20.
50. Tom Brass, "Latin American Peasants."
51. James Petras and Henry Veltmeyer, "Are Latin American Peasant Movements Still a Force for Change? Some New Paradigms Revisited," *Journal of Peasant Studies* 28, no. 2 (2001): 83118.
52. See the report by the State Statistical Bureau in China, http://www.stats.gov.cn/tjsj/zxfb/201704/t20170428_1489334.html.
53. J. B. Foster, R. W. McChesney, and R. J. Jonna, "The Global Reserve Army of Labor and the New Imperialism," *Monthly Review* 63, no. 6 (2011), 1–3.

Chapter 3: Agricultural Productivity and Decollectivization

1. Officially the land was contracted to households for fifteen years, but the contract got extended again and again, and in de facto terms the land was privatized with a temporarily but highly regulated land market.
2. B. Stone, "Developments in Agricultural Technology," *China Quarterly*, no. 116 (1988): 767822.
3. Ibid.
4. Ibid.
5. Take rural water electricity stations, for example: the total capacity increased from 20,000 kilowatts in 1957 to 2.28 million kilowatts in 1978 (Ministry of Agriculture 2009, 7).

6. For the pros and cons of increased intensity, see Philip C. Huang, *The Peasant Family and Rural Development in the Yangzi Delta, 1350–1988* (Stanford, CA: Stanford University Press, 1990).
7. Based on later years' data from the Ministry of Agriculture (2009: 6, 17), the cropping index was 1.55 in 1990 and 1.58 in 1994; after 1994 the size of cultivated land was adjusted to increase, and therefore the index went down structurally: in 2008 it was 1.28.
8. Funing Zhong, *The Political Economy of the Chinese Grain Marketing System* (Canberra: Australian National University, 2004).
9. Ibid.
10. For example, see Table A1 in T. Sicular, "Agricultural Planning and Pricing in the Post-Mao Period," *China Quarterly*, no. 116 (1988): 671–705.
11. See, for example, Guanzhong James Wen, "Total Factor Productivity Change in China's Farming Sector: 1952–1989," *Economic Development and Cultural Change* 42, no. 1 (1993): 1–41; Shenggen Fan and Xiaobo Zhang, "Production and Productivity Growth in Chinese Agriculture: New National and Regional Measures," *Economic Development and Cultural Change* 50, no. 4 (2002): 819–838.
12. K. P. Kalirajan, M. B. Obwona, and S. Zhao, "A Decomposition of Total Factor Productivity Growth: The Case of Chinese Agricultural Growth Before and After Reforms," *American Journal of Agricultural Economics* 78, no. 2 (1996): 331–338.
13. Louis Putterman provides a detailed explanation and comparisons among this type of work. See chapter 7 in *Continuity and Change in China's Rural Development* (New York: Oxford University Press, 1993).
14. John McMillan, John Whalley, and Lijing Zhu, "The Impact of China's Economic Reforms on Agricultural Productivity Growth," *Journal of Political Economy* 97, no. 4 (1989): 781–807.
15. Interestingly, the reasons they provided for not considering technical progress was because "Chinese agriculture had already attained a technically advanced state before the period examined here."
16. Carol Carolus, *Sources of Chinese Agricultural Growth in the 1980s* (Boston: Boston University Press, 1992).
17. Carl Riskin, *China's Political Economy: The Quest for Development Since 1949* (New York: Oxford University Press, 1987).
18. Chris Bramall, *Sources of Chinese Economic Growth, 1978–1996* (New York: Oxford University Press, 2000).
19. Dongping Han, *The Unknown Cultural Revolution: Life and Change in a Chinese Village* (New York: Monthly Revlew Press, 2008).
20. Chris Bramall, "Origins of the Agricultural 'Miracle': Some Evidence from Sichuan," *China Quarterly*, no. 143 (1995): 731–755.
21. Louis Putterman, "Entering the Post-Collective Era in North China: Dahe Township," *Modern China* 15, no. 3 (1989): 275–320.
22. Huang, *The Peasant Family and Rural Development*, 222–251.

23. Justin Yifu Lin, "Rural Reforms and Agricultural Growth in China," *American Economic Review* 82, no. 1 (1992): 34–51.
24. I downloaded Lin's original dataset from Lin's development forum, http://jlin.ccer.edu.cn/. This page is not available anymore, so if needed please contact me to get a copy of the dataset.
25. Bramall, *Sources of Chinese Economic Growth*, 329.
26. Calculated based on State Statistical Bureau (2005, section 38).
27. There are different measures of the size of cultivated land. It is normally believed that the official statistics in the 1970s and 1980s largely underestimated the land size; however, this does not change the fact that the cultivated land decreased at a higher rate after the rural reform. In fact, the recent data suggests that the land size kept increasing before 1980 and started declining after 1980 (Bi and Zheng, 2000).
28. The calculations are based on Ministry of Agriculture (2009, 5).
29. Bramall, *Sources of Chinese Economic Growth*, 247.
30. Stone, "Developments in Agricultural Technology."

Chapter 4: The Political Economy of Decollectivization

1. Excerpts from Deng Xiaoping's talks given in Wuchang, Shenzhen, Zhuhai, and Shanghai, January 18–February 21, 1992. Published in *Selected Works of Deng Xiaoping*, vol. 3 (Beijing: Renmin Chubanshe, 1993), 370–383.
2. For example, see the Communiqué of the Third Plenary of the 15th Central Committee of the CCP, October 14, 1998, http://cpc.people.com.cn (in Chinese).
3. This was suggested by many writings: for example, Justin Yifu Lin, "The Household Responsibility System in China's Agricultural Reform: A Theoretical and Empirical Study," *Economic Development and Cultural Change* 36, no. 3 (1988): S199–S224; Daniel Kelliher, *Peasant Power in China* (New Haven, CT: Yale University Press, 1992); K. X. Zhou, *How the Farmers Changed China: Power of the People* (Boulder, CO: Westview Press, 1996). A typical Chinese text is Liqun Ma and Zhijun Lin, *Jiaofeng* (Crossing Swords). Beijing: (Jin Ri Zhongguo Chu Ban She), 1998.
4. Chris Bramall, *Sources of Chinese Economic Growth, 1978–1996* (New York: Oxford University Press, 2000), 330.
5. *Bashi niandai chu di wo guo nongye shengchan ze ren zhi: Diaocha baogao xuanbian* [Selected reports on China's agriculture responsibility system] (Beijing: Hongqi Chuban She, 1984).
6. Shanghai Nongyezhi Committee, *Shanghai nongyezhi* [Shanghai agriculture records] (Shanghai: Shanghai Shehui Kexueyuan Chubanshe, 1996), 35–36.
7. Beijing Difangzhi Committee, *Beijingzhi: nongyejuan nongcun jingji zonghezhi* [Beijing rural economic records] (Beijing: Chubanshe, 2008), 545–559.
8. Yunnan Difangzhi Committee, *Yunnan Shengzhi nongyezhi* [Yunnan

agricultural records] (Kunming: Yunnan Renmin Chubanshe, 1998), 138–139.

9. Zhejiang Nongyezhi Committee, *Zhejiangsheng nongyezhi* [Zhejiang agricultural records] (Bejing: Zhonghua Shuju, 2004), 192–198.
10. Hunan Difangzhi Committee, *Hunanshengzhi nonglinshuilizhi* [*Hunan agriculture records*] (Changsha: Hunan Chubanshe, 1991), 53–57.
11. Du Runsheng, *Du Rusheng zishu*, 130–131.
12. Ibid., 131.
13. This is confirmed in Hu Yaobang's son's recollection, available at http://history.gmw.cn/2011- 09/27/content_2704616_4.htm, accessed on March 2, 2016.
14. David Zweig, "Opposition to Change in Rural China: The System of Responsibility and People's Communes," *Asian Survey* 23, no. 7 (1983): 879–900; Kathleen Hartford, "Socialist Agriculture Is Dead: Long Live Socialist Agriculture! Organizational Transformation in Rural China," in Elizabeth Perry and Christine Wong, eds., *The Political Economy of Reform in PostMao China: Causes, Content, and Consequences* (Cambridge, MA: Harvard University Press, 1985); William Hinton, *The Great Reversal* (New York: Monthly Review Press, 1990); Bramall, *Sources of Chinese Economic Growth*; Tongxue Tan, "Zhuanxing xiangcun de daode, quanli yu shehui jiegou (Morality, Power, and Social Structure in the Transition of Rural Society)" (PhD diss., Huazhong University of Science and Technology, 2007); Han, *The Unknown Cultural Revolution*.
15. Kelliher, *Peasant Power in China*, 105.
16. See Huang, *The Spiral Road*, 162–173.
17. He, Xuefeng. "Renmin gongshe de sanda gongneng" [Three functions of the People's Commune]. http://www.snzg.cn/artlcle/2007/1114/artlcle_7916.html, accessed on Dec 29, 2011.
18. Zhou, *How the Farmers Changed China*.
19. Fujian Difangzhi Committee, *Fujianshengzhi gongchandangzhi* [Fujian Communist Party records] (Beijing: Zhongguo Shehui Kexue Chubanshe, 1999), 189–192; Hunan Difangzhi Committee, *Hunanshengzhi nonglinshuilizhi*, 53–57.
20. Reported in Hartford, "Socialist Agriculture Is Dead," 39.
21. Anita Chan, Richard Madsen, and Jonathan Unger, *Chen Village Under Mao and Deng* (Berkeley: Unlversity of Callfornla Press, 1992), 271.
22. Thomas Bernstein, "Farmer Discontent and Regime Responses," in Merle Goldman and Roderlck Macfarquhar, eds., *The Paradox of China's Post-Mao Reforms* (Cambridge, MA: Harvard University Press, 1999), 197–219.
23. Lin, "Rural Reforms and Agricultural Growth in China"; Kelliher, *Peasant Power in China*.
24. This phrase might have its origin from Heilongjiang Province; see Zhenqi Wang, "Huyaobang yanli piping 'dingmengang' " [Hu Yaobang harshly criticizes "blocks"], *Shi Ji Qiao* 12 (2011): 45–47. As David Kotz and Sigrid

Schmalzer suggested, this kind of phrase was also used in China during the eras of Mao and the Soviet Union.
25. Hartford, "Socialist Agriculture Is Dead."
26. Zweig, "Opposition to Change in Rural China."
27. Han, *The Unknown Cultural Revolution*, 156.
28. Shi Bai, "Wo cong fuchuji yibu kuajin shengwei changwei" [Huge Promotion to provincial standing committee], *Yanhuang Chunqiu* no. 7 (2007): 6–11.
29. Zweig, "Opposition to Change in Rural China."
30. Ibid: Bramall, "Origins of the Agricultural 'Miracle.'"
31. Roderick MacFarquhar, "The Succession to Mao and the End of Maoism, 1969–82," in R. MacFarquhar, ed., *The Politics of China: The Eras of Mao and Deng* (Cambridge, UK: Cambridge University Press, 1997), 248–339.
32. Huang, *The Spiral Road*, 162–173.
33. Han, *The Unknown Cultural Revolution*, 158–159.
34. Du Runsheng recounts this story. An old leftist cadre came to Wan Li (who was then governor of Anhui Province) in a meeting, saying that decollectivization is not egalitarian and not achieving socialism. Wan fought back with the question, "Socialism or people, which do you want?" The poor man immediately replied: "Socialism!" Wan said, "I want people." See *Du Rusheng zishu* [Du Runsheng's recollections] (Beijing: Renmin Chubanshe, 2005), 126.
35. Zhou, *How the Farmers Changed China*, 67.
36. MacFarquhar, "The Succession to Mao," and confirmed by Zhao Ziyang himself; see Zhao Ziyang, *Gaige licheng* [The secret journal of Zhao Ziyang] (Hong Kong: Xinshiji Chubanshe, 2009), 138. Deng's talk on rural policy was given in May 1980; it was later published in *Xiaoping wenxuan*, vol. 1 (Beijing: Renmin Chubanshe, 1962/1994), 316.
37. Huang, *The Spiral Road*, 162–173.
38. Jilin Difangzhi Committee, *Jilinshengzhi: Nongyezhi* [Jilin agricultural records] (Jinlin: Renmln Chubanshe, 1993), 478–483.
39. Wang Yanhai, "Kuachu diyibu hao Jianxin" [Hard to take the first step] *Jianghuai Wenshi* no. 4 (2007): 117–129.
40. Maurice Meisner, *Mao's China and After: A History of the People's Republic* (New York: Free Press, 1999), 463.
41. The novel was written by Caiqin Zhou. It got the national award for excellent short novels in 1981, which was the most important literature award in the early 1980s.
42. Deng Xiaoping, "Emancipate the Mind, Seek Truth from Facts and Unite as One in Looking to the Future," in Deng, *Selected Works of Deng Xiaoping*. Originally December 1978.
43. Ibid.
44. See the *People's Daily* editorial, "Jiakuai nongye fazhan de qiangda dongli" [The Force of Accelerating Agricultural Development], October 7, 1979, http://cpc.people.com.cn.

45. "Guanyu jianguo yilal dang de ruogan lishi wentl de jueyi" [Resolutlons on some hlstorical issues of CCP], from the CCP 11th Central Committee 6th Plenary, 1981, http://cpc.people.com.cn.
46. Suinian Liu and Wu Qungan, *Wenhuadageming shiqi de guominjingji* [The economy during the Cultural Revolution] (Harbin: Heilongjiang Renmin Chubanshe, 1986), 109; Du Runsheng, ed., *Dangdai zhongguo de nongye hezuozhi* [Collective agriculture in modern China] (Beijing: Dangdai Zhongguo Chubanshe, 2002), 722.
47. Hu Yaobang's report to the CCP 12th National Congress may be viewed online at http://cpc.people.com.cn/GB/64162/64168/64565/65448/45264 30.html.
48. Du Runsheng, "Nongcun gongzuo de lishi zhuanbian" [Historical transformation of rural management], *People's Daily*, September 16, 1982.
49. Yu Jiafu, "Zhao Ziyang huijian mei jingjixuejia shuerci shi shuo, zhongguo nongye jixu fazhan xuyao houxu zhengce" [Zhao Ziyan claims Chinese agriculture need more policy support in his meeting with T. Shultz], *People's Daily*, May 17, 1988.
50. Du Runsheng, "Yikao kexue jishu zengqiang nongye jingji diwei" [Rely on technology, improve agricultural economy], *People's Daily*, April 11, 1986.
51. From the *People's Daily* (overseas edition), June 12, 1986; cited in note 1 of D. Y. Hsu and P.Y. Ching, "The Worker-Peasant Alliance as a Strategy for Rural Development in China," *Monthly Review*, 42, no. 10 (March 1991): 27–43.
52. Hsu and Ching, "The Worker-Peasant Alliance."
53. See "Jiangzemin zai guoqing sishi zhounian dahui shang de jianghua" [Jiang Zemin's Speech for the 40th Anniversary of the People's Republic of China], *People's Daily*, September 30,1989.
54. Wu Rong, "Wei zhongyang nongyanshi dagong" [Working for the Central Agriculture Research Bureau], *Zhongshan Fengyu*, no. 3 (2008): 20–22.
55. Communiqué of the Third Plenary of the 15th Central Committee of the CCP, October 14, 1998, http://cpc.people.com.cn.
56. For example, Du Runsheng, "Lian chan chengbao zhi he nongcun hezuo jingji de xin fazhan" [Responsibility system and new development of rural cooperatives], *People's Daily*, March 7, 1983.
57. See http://cpc.people.com.cn/GB/64162/64168/64569/65411/4429165.html and http://cpc.people.com.cn/GB/64093/64094/8194418.html for the resolutions at the 16th and 17th Central Committee reports, respectively.
58. Meisner, *Mao's China and After*, 430–432.
59. Ibid.
60. "Resolutions on Some Historical Issues of CCP" from CCP 11th Central Committee 6th Plenary, 1981.
61. Deng Xiaoping, "Emancipate the Mind, Seek Truth from Facts and Unite as One in Looking to the Future," December 1978, republished in Deng, *Selected Works*, 1984.
62. Meisner, *Mao's China and After*, 470.

63. For grains, quota price increased by 20 percent and above-quota price increased by 50 percent; see Terry Sicular, "Agricultural Planning and Pricing in the Post-Mao Period," *China Quarterly* 116 (1988): 671–705.
64. Jiang Zilong, "Qiaochangzhang shangren ji" [Qiao became the new director], in *1979 Nian quanguo youxiu duanpian xiaoshuo pingxuan huojiang zuopin ji* [1979 Selection of the awarded short novels], ed. Renmin Wenxue (Shanghai: Shanghai Wenyi Chubanshe, 1979).
65. Jiang Zilong, "Zihao yu beiqing: yige laogongren de shushuo" [Pride and sorrow: A recollection of an old worker], *Tong zhou gong jin*, no. 8 (2010): 14–17.
66. MacFarquhar, "The Succession to Mao and the End of Maoism, 1969–82."
67. The earlier urban reform, sometimes described as *Yang Yue Jin* [Import Great Leap Forward], in which some very expensive machinery was imported to build new factories.
68. Meisner, *Mao's China and After*, 470.
69. Ibid., 471.
70. Jinglian Wu, "20 Nian lai gaige lilun de fazhan" [20 Years' development of the theory of reform], Z. Zhang, F. Huang and G. Li, *20 Nian jingji gaige huigu yu zhanwang* [20 Years of economic reform: retrospect and prospect] (Beijing: Zhongguo Jihua Chuban She, 1998).
71. Meisner, *Mao's China and After*, 471; Wu, "Wei zhongyang nongyanshi dagong."
72. Du Runsheng, "Nongcun shengchan zerenzhi yu nngcun jingji tizhi gaige" [The rural responsibility system and rural economic reform], *Hongqi* no. 19 (1981): 383.
73. Sulamith Potter and Jack Potter, *China's Peasants: The Anthropology of a Revolution* (Cambridge, UK: Cambridge University Press, 1990), 158–179.
74. Calculated based on State Statistical Bureau (2005, section 3, 39).
75. Hinton, *The Great Reversal*.
76. See the critique of decollectivization in "Jie chuan baochan daohu zhen mianmu" [Revealing the true nature of decollectivization], *People's Daily*, November 2, 1959.
77. Most political bulletins and pamphlets on agriculture at that time termed all the decollectivization measures as some kind of "responsibility system" under socialism. For example, see Xiang Wu, "Yang guan dao yu du mu qiao: Shi tan baochan daohu de youlai libi xingzhi he qianjing" [Big lanes and small bridges: The nature of decollectivization], *People's Daily*, November 5, 1980.
78. Wu, "Twenty Years' Development of the Theory of Reform."
79. For example, see Wu Xiang, "Yang guan dao yu du mu qiao" [Shining road and single-log bridge], *People's Daily*, November 5, 1980; Du Runsheng, "Nongcun shengchan zerenzhi yu nngcun jingji tizhi gaige" [The rural responsibility system and rural economic reform], *Hongqi* no. 19 (1981): 383.
80. The CCP's resolution on economic structural reform, made at the Third

Plenary of the 12th Central Committee on October 20, 1984, is available at http://cpc.people.com.cn.
81. Bernstein, "Farmer Discontent and Regime Responses."
82. Ibid.
83. Clemens Stubbe-Østergaard, "Introduction," in *Remaking Peasant China: Problems of Rural Development and Institutions at the Start of the 1990s*, J. Delman, C. Stubbe-Østergaard, and F. Christiansen, eds. (Denmark: Aarhus University Press, 1990).
84. Bernstein, "Farmer Discontent and Regime Responses."
85. Mao repeated this many times. See Pang Xianzhi and Jin Chongji, eds., *Maozedong Zhuan* [A biography of Mao Zedong: 1949–1976] (Beijing: Zhongyang Wenxian Chubanshe, 2003), chap. 30.

Chapter 5: The Political Economy of Decollectivization

1. For an excellent explanation of the commune structure, see Potter and Potter, *China's Peasants*.
2. Interviews with Person #28 (February 5, 2011), Person #19 (January 20, 2011).
3. Li had interesting discussions on the peasants' strategies under the different systems; see Huaiyin Li, "Everyday Strategies for Team Farming in Collective-era China: Evidence from Qin Village," *China Journal* 54 (2005): 79–98.
4. Interviews with Person #32, Person #25 (February 10, 2011).
5. Songzi Xianzhi Committee, *Songzi xianzhi* [Local records of Songzi, 1949–1985] (Songzi: Songzi Xianzhi Committee, 1986), 286–287.
6. Ibid., 290–292.
7. Ibid., 293–294.
8. It is worth mentioning that, due to lack of data for 1956, the record harvest of 1957 was used as the beginning of the collective era; this might lead to an underestimate of the overall improvement.
9. Songzi Water Bureau, *Songzi shuilizhi* [History of water utilization] (Beijing: Zhongguo Huanjing Kexue Chubanshe, 2008), 49–53; Songzi Xianzhi Committee, *Songzi xianzhi*, 59.
10. Songzi Xianzhi Committee, *Songzi xianzhi*, 551.
11. Ibid., 560.
12. Ibid., 553.
13. Ibid. Middle school and high school education saw similar expansion, although the most significant improvements happened later, during the Cultural Revolution.
14. Ibid., 561.
15. Ibid.
16. See similar observations in Dongping Han, *The Unknown Cultural Revolution: Life and Change in a Chinese Village* (New York: Monthly Review Press, 2008).
17. Songzi Xianzhi Committee, *Songzi xianzhi*, 653.

18. Ibid.
19. Ibid., 62.
20. Xizhe Peng, "Demographic Consequences of the Great Leap Forward in China's Provinces," *Population and Development Review* 13, no. 4 (1987): 639–670; Carl Riskin, "Seven Questions About the Chinese Famine of 1959–1961," *China Economic Review* 9, no. 2 (1998): 111–124.
21. For this talk, "Yong shishi shuohua" [Speak with facts], see Deng, *Deng Xiaoping wenxuan*, vol. 2, 155–156.
22. Louis Putterman, "Ration Subsidies and Incentives in the Pre-Reform Chinese Commune," *Economica* 55, no. 218 (1988): 235–247; Du, *Du Rusheng Zishu*, 133; James Kaising Kung, "Egalitarianism, Subsistence Provision, and Work Incentives in China's Agricultural Collectives," *World Development* 22, no. 2 (1994): 175–187.
23. Lin, "The Household Responsibility System in China's Agricultural Reform."
24. Carl Riskin. "Maoism and Motivation: Work Incentives in China," in *China's Uninterrupted Revolution*, edited by Victor Nee and James Peck, (New York: Pantheon Books), 415–461.
25. This is the impression from all the interviews.
26. Interview with Person #8, Person #17 (January 12, 2011), Person #18 (January 27, 2011), Person #23 (February 2, 2011), Person #12 (18 January 18, 2011).
27. This was confirmed by all the people interviewed.
28. Huaiyin Li, "Everyday Strategies for Team Farming in Collective-era China: Evidence from Qin Village," *China Journal* 54 (2015): 79–98.
29. Interview with Person #17 (January 13, 2011), Person #34 (January 11, 2011).
30. Commission of the Central Committee of the CPSU(B), *History of Communist Party of Soviet Union (Bolsheviks)*. (New York: International Publishers, 1939), 316.
31. Mao Zedong, *Maozedong du shehuizhuyi zhengzhijingjixue pizhu he tanhua* [Mao on Socialist Political Economy, 1998] zhonghua renmin gongheguo guoshi xuehui, 248.
32. Interview with Person #24 (February 5, 2011).
33. Carl Riskin, "Maoism and Motivation: Work Incentives in China." In *China's Uninterrupted Revolution*, edited by Victor Nee and James Peck, (New York: Pantheon Books, 1975), 415–461.
34. Interviews with Person #19 (January 20, 2011), Person #3 (January 14, 2011), Person #14, Person #8 (January 12, 2011).
35. Interview with Person #33 (January 24, 2011).
36. Person #23 (February 2, 2011).
37. Interviews with Person #9, Person #11 (January 10, 2011), Person #17 (January 11, 2011), Person #18 (January 27, 2011), Person #25 (February 10, 2011).
38. Potter and Potter, *China's Peasants*, 102.

39. Huaiyin Li, *Village China Under Socialism and Reform: A Micro History, 1948—2008* (Stanford, CA: Stanford University Press, 2009), 135.
40. Interview with Person #17 (January 13, 2011)
41. Zhengwen Yang, "Di si ci Diaocha" [The fourth investigation], *Liao Wang Zhou Kan* no. 08 (1984): 26–27.
42. William Hinton, *Fanshen: A Documentary of Revolution in a Chinese Village* (London:Vintage Books, 1966), 222–231.
43. William Hinton, *Shenfan: The Continuing Revolution in a Chinese Village* (New York: Random House, 1983), 665–674.
44. Interview with Person #27 (February 22, 2011).
45. Interview with Person #6 (December 28, 2010).
46. Interviews with Person #33 (January 24, 2011), Person #24 (February 3, 2011).
47. Interview with Person #27 (February 22, 2011).
48. Han, *The Unknown Cultural Revolution*.
49. This answer was given by all the people interviewed.
50. U.S. Department of Agriculture, "Agricultural Statistics of the People's Republic of China, 1949–90," Robinson Rojas Archive, 1992, Table 216–8, http://www.rrojasdatabank.info/90010.htm; accessed February 20, 2014.
51. Songzi Xianzhi Committee, *Songzi xianzhi*, 60, 288.
52. Ibid., 60
53. Ashwani Saith, "From Collectives to Markets: Restructured Agriculture-Industry Linkages in Rural China; Some Micro-level Evidence," *Journal of Peasant Studies* 22, no. 2 (1995): 201–260.
54. Ashwani Saith, "China and India: The Institutional Roots of Differential Performance," *Development and Change* 39, no. 5 (2008): 723–757.
55. Interview with Person #4 (January 28, 2011).
56. Martin King Whyte, "Inequality and Stratification in China," *China Quarterly* 64 (1975): 684–711.
57. Calculation based on data from Songzi Xianzhi Committee, *Songzi xianzhi*, 538.
58. Paul A. Baran, *The Political Economy of Growth* (New York: Monthly Review Press, 1962), xxxv.
59. Whyte, "Inequality and Stratification in China."
60. Marc Blecher, "Income Distribution in Small Rural Chinese Communities," *China Quarterly* 68 (1976): 797–816.
61. Keith Griffin and Ashwani Saith, "The Pattern of Income Inequality in Rural China," *Oxford Economic Papers* 34, no. 1 (1982): 172–206.
62. E. B. Vermeer, "Income Differentials in Rural China," *China Quarterly* 89 (1982): 1–33.
63. Jonathan Unger, "The Decollectivization of the Chinese Countryside: A Survey of Twenty-eight Villages," *Pacific Affairs* 58, no. 4 (1985): 585–606.
64. The story below is taken from Du (2005: 132–134).
65. This was confirmed by all the older peasants interviewed.
66. Interviews with Person #1, Person #12, Person #13 (January 18, 2011),

Person #25 (January 15, 2011).
67. Interview with Person #13 (January 18, 2011).
68. Interview with Person #14 (January 12, 2011).
69. Interview with Person #22 (January 17, 2011).
70. Interviews with Person #17 (January 11, 2011), Person #9 (January 10, 2011), Person #20 (January 22, 2011), Person #33 (January 24, 2011), Person #18 (January 27, 2011).
71. Even relatively recently, a local author—a longtime rural cadre himself—published a novel along these lines; see Tian Yonghua, *Chun feng man juan* [Spring winds come] (Wuhan: Changjiang Wenyi Chubanshe, 2008). The book had a somewhat unnuanced storyline: the procollective leader (who had the usual negative features of a villain) was in power; production was in a mess and the leader took advantage of a young girl when her lover went out. With the support of the masses, the girl's lover, who was anti-collective, defeated the evil leader and dismantled the collective.
72. Interview with Person #14 (January 12, 2011).
73. Interview with Person #3 (January 13, 2011).
74. Interview with Person #17 (January 12, 2011).
75. Interviews with Person #7, Person #15, Person #31 (January 13, 2011).
76. Interviews with Person #7, #15, #31 (January 13, 2011).
77. Saith, "From Collectives to Markets."
78. E. Friedman, P. G. Pickowicz, and M. Selden, *Revolution, Resistance, and Reform in Village China* (New Haven, CT: Yale University Press, 2007), 276–279.
79. For some background on the Wukan incident, see "Inside Wukan: The Chinese Village That Fought Back," by M. Moore, *The Telegraph*, December 13, 2011, http://www.telegraph.co.uk/news/worldnews/asia/china/8954315/Inside-Wukan-the-Chinese-village-that-fought-back.html.

Index

agrarian question, Du on, 33–34
agrarian reform, *See* land reform
agribusiness, 24
agricultural machinery, 42, 54
agriculture: during Cultural Revolution, 66; green revolution in, 24, 42; impact of HRS on productivity of, 52–55; productivity of, 39; in Songzi collectives, 83–84; technology for, 30
Allende, Salvador, 20
Alliance for Progress, 20
Anhui Province (China), 64, 73
Arbenz, Jacobo, 20

Babao Commune, 101
Badiou, Alain, 111–12
Baran, Paul, 103
Beijing (China), 59, 61
Bernstein, Thomas, 61–62

Bo Yibo, 104
Bramall, Chris, 48–49, 59
Brass, Tom, 35, 36
Breaking with Old Ideas (Juelie; film), 31–32
brigades, 81, 82

cadres: during decollectivization, 106; in political stratification, 93–97; state under control of, 31
capitalism: in agrarian question, 25, 28, 30, 34–35; in Chinese countryside, 110–11; in post-Mao urban reforms, 70–72
capitalist class: in current China, 37; land reform and, 20–22, 24
Carolus, Carol, 48, 49, 51
Chan, Anita, 61
chemical fertilizers, 41–42, 54–55
Chen Village (China), 30
Chile, 20

China: agrarian question in, 25–29; agrarian reform in, 20; great famine in, 90; revival of Marxism in, 110; state machine in, 30–31; two periods in history of, 11
Chinese Communist Party (CCP): after death of Mao, 32; debates within, 13–14; on decollectivization, 16, 59, 66–68, 73–74, 104–5; decollectivization as decision of, 60–62; on end of class struggle, 69; factions within, 29–30; under Mao, 28; peasants and, 26, 27; reforms reversed by, 12; on rural development, 35; urban reform by, 71–72
Chinese Revolution (1949), 38
Ching, P.Y., 67
class struggle, 69, 77
collectivization and collectives, 24–28; agriculture in, 83–84; contradictions within, 89–90; dismantling of, 39; education in, 86–88; health in, 88–89; infrastructure of, 84–86; institutions and achievements of, 81–82; opponents of, 79–80; political stratification within, 95–99; pro-accumulation policies of, 99–104; stratification and efficiency in, 90–95; transition period leading to decollectivization, 40–46
communes, 81, 82
Communist Party (China), *See* Chinese Communist Party

Communist Party (Soviet Union), 93
cotton, 83, 84
Cuba: agrarian reform in, 20; private agricultural markets in, 22
Cultural Revolution: agriculture during, 66; condemnations of, 69; education during, 87; political struggles during, 98–99; state machine during, 31

da bao gan, 74
debt crisis, 24
debts, 100–102
decollectivization, 7, 8; CCP favoring, 15–16; in China, 26, 28–29; conditions for, 68–75; after death of Mao, 32–34; migrations caused by, 36; myths of, 58–65; in neoliberal doctrine, 109; political consequences of, 75–77; political economy of, 57–58; production increase attributed to, 15; in Songzi County, 104–7; transition period leading to, 40–46; *See also* household responsibility system
democracy: in control of state, 37–38; in rural collectives, 95–96
Deng Xiaoping: agricultural policies of, 12; on decollectivization, 29, 57, 63, 68; on egalitarianism, 90; market reforms advocated by, 65–66; on modernization, 70; on peasants, 76; takes power, 69

Index

Deng Zihui, 27, 28
Dongping Han, 99
Du Runsheng: on agricultural technology, 67; as head of National Agricultural Committee, 33–34; on left opposition, 66; on reform of rural collectives, 104; on shifts in provincial leadership, 60

education, 86–88
egalitarianism, 90, 103
Egypt, 20, 25
elites, in China, 31

famine (1959-1961), 14, 90
fertilizers, 41–42, 54–55
floods and droughts, 84
food: demand within China for, 37; during great famine, 90; patterns in consumption of, 99
Friedman, E., 107
Friedman, Milton, 24
Fujian Province (China), 61

grain production, 14–15, 24, 29, 99
great famine (1959-1961), 14, 90
green revolution, 24, 42
Guatemala, 20

Han, Dongping, 48, 62, 63
health, in Songzi County, 88–89
Hebei Province (China), 60, 62
The Herdsman (*Mu Ma Ren;* film), 32
He Shiguang, 105
He Xuefeng, 61

Hinton, William, 8, 72, 97
household contract and performance-based compensation and responsibility system, 41
household production system, 39–40
household responsibility system (HRS), 41; assessments of, 46–55; changed to responsibility system, 67–68; transition period leading to, 40–46; *See also* decollectivization
Hsu, D.Y., 67
Hua Guofeng, 69
Huaiyin Li, 95–96
Huang, Shumin, 61, 63, 64
Hunan Province (China), 60
Hu Yaobang, 59, 60, 66
hybrid crops, 54; rice, 42, 83

income inequality, 103–4
indebtedness in rural collectives, 100–102
India, 21
infrastructure, in Songzi County, 84–86, 100
intellectuals, 69

Jiangxi Province (China), 61
Jiang Zemin, 67
Jiang Zilong, 70–71
Jilin Province (China), 64
Jimo County (China), 62

land reform (agrarian reform), 11–12, 19–24
Lao Tian, 110

Latin America: land reform in, 20–21, 24; peasant movements in, 35–36
Lenin, V. I., 30
lianchan, 74
lianchanzerenzhi (performance-based compensation and responsibility system), 41
Lin, Justin, 15, 46, 53; replications of work of, 49–52
Liu Shaoqi, 26–29
Longbow Village (China), 97

MacFarquhar, Roderick, 63, 71
Madsen, Richard, 61
Mao Zedong, 8, 11, 12; on cadres and workers, 93; after Chinese Revolution, 38; on class struggle, 77; collectivization under, 27–29; condemnations of, 69; Cultural Revolution under, 31; death of, 32, 65; in debates within CCP, 14; on inequality, 30; on peasants, 26
Marxism, 110
McMillan, John, 47–48
Meisner, Maurice, 69
Mexico, 22
migration, caused by decollectivization, 36
modernization, 20, 69–70
multiple cropping index (MCI), 44, 53

neoliberal capitalist program, 14; in China, 32–36; decollectivization in, 109; resistance to, 111
neoliberalism, 19

peasants: in agrarian question, 25; as allies of land reform, 20–22; during Chinese collectivization, 26–28; collectives dissolved by, 58; during Cultural Revolution, 99; debts of, 100–102; during decollectivization, 105–7; during land reform, 24; in Latin America, 35–36; power lost by, 75–76, 111; in Songzi, collectives for, 81; work avoidance by, 90–91
Peng, Zhaochang, 8
People's Food Sovereignty (Chinese website), 110
performance-based compensation and responsibility system *(lianchanzerenzhi)*, 41
Peru, 20–21
Petras, James, 35–36
political stratification, 95–99
population, 72, 99–100
populist program, 14; in agrarian question, 25, 28, 30, 34, 35; after Mao's death, 33
Potter, Jack, 72, 95
Potter, Sulamith, 72, 95
poverty, 99
privatization, 74, 109
pro-accumulation policies, 99–104
production teams, 81–82
productivity, 93–95
public health, 88–89
Putterman, Louis, 49

Index

rapeseed (canola oil), 83–84
responsibility system *(zerenzhi)*, 41, 67–68, 73–74; *See also* household responsibility system
rice: hybrid, 42; price of, 102; in Songzi County, 83
Riskin, Carl, 48, 94
rural collectives, *See* collectivization and collectives
Russia, 22

Saint-Simon, Henri de, 26
sanziyibao, 29
schools, 87
sexual relationships, 96–97
Shaanxi Province (China), 62
Shanghai (China), 59
Shan yue bu zhi xin li shi (novel), 64–65
She Shui Nong Fu, 110
socialism, 38; in agrarian question, 25, 28–30, 35; in organization of work, 94
socialist countries, rising elites in, 22
Songzi County (China), 80; agriculture in, 83–84; decollectivization in, 104–7; education in, 86–88; infrastructure in, 84–86; organization of collectives in, 81–83; political stratification in, 95–99; pro-accumulation policies in, 99–104; stratification and efficiency in, 90–95
South Korea, 19, 22
Soviet Union, 19, 21; collapse of, 22; collectivization in, 24, 28; privatization of agriculture in, 25
state: Chinese, 30–31; democratic control of, 37–38
stratification, 16–17; decollectivization and, 106–7; political, 95–99; work avoidance and, 90–95

Taiwan, 19, 21, 22
Tanzania, 22
technology: agricultural production and, 30; during transition period, 41–44, 54–55
Thatcher, Margaret, 22
Tian Jiyun, 67
tong gou tong xiao (unified procurement and marketing policy), 44–45
total-factor productivity (TFP), 46–47
transition period, 40–46

Unger, Jonathan, 61
unified procurement and marketing policy *(tong gou tong xiao)*, 44–45
urban China, 70–72

Veltmeyer, Henry, 35–36

Wang Yanhai, 64
water management, in Songzi County, 84–86
weather, 42–44, 52, 53
Weishui Reservoir, 86
Wen Tiejun, 34, 36

Whalley, John, 47–48
Whyte, Martin King, 103
women, 96–97
work avoidance, 90–95
working class, 36, 111
work points, 82, 91, 96
Wu Jinglian, 71
Wukan (China), 107

Xiliu Village (China), 96–97, 107

Yang Chuanrong, 96–97

Yunnan Province (China), 59

zerenzhi (responsibility system), 41
Zhao Ziyang, 63, 67
Zhejiang Province (China), 60
Zhidan County (China), 62
Zhou, Kate Xiao, 61, 63
Zhou Xianyin, 96–97, 107
Zhu, Lijing, 47–48
Zhu Rongji, 34
Zweig, David, 62